Popular Mech

BY CHRIS PETERSON

# HOW TO CARVE A TURKEY
## AND 99 OTHER SKILLS EVERY MAN SHOULD KNOW

**HEARST BOOKS**
A division of Sterling Publishing Co., Inc.

New York / London
**www.sterlingpublishing.com**

Book design by DesignWorks
Edited by Sarah Scheffel
For art credits, see page 184.

Library of Congress Cataloging-in-Publication Data is available.

10  9  8  7  6  5  4  3  2  1

Published by Hearst Books
A division of Sterling Publishing Co., Inc.
387 Park Avenue South, New York, NY 10016

Popular Mechanics and Hearst Books are trademarks of Hearst Communications, Inc.

www.popularmechanics.com

For information about custom editions, special sales, premium and corporate purchases, please contact Sterling Special Sales Department at 800-805-5489 or specialsales@sterlingpublishing.com.

Distributed in Canada by Sterling Publishing
c/o Canadian Manda Group, 165 Dufferin Street
Toronto, Ontario, Canada M6K 3H6

Distributed in Australia by Capricorn Link (Australia) Pty. Ltd.
P.O. Box 704, Windsor, NSW 2756 Australia

Manufactured in China

Sterling ISBN: 978-1-58816-753-8

Popular Mechanics

# HOW TO CARVE A TURKEY
## AND 99 OTHER SKILLS EVERY MAN SHOULD KNOW

# CONTENTS

# INTRODUCTION

**P**opular Mechanics' readers aren't couch jockeys. It's always been part of the magazine's mission to empower men—and women, for that matter—to go and do whatever it is they want to go and do. Since the start more than a hundred years ago, we've been all about taking action, and our articles have always offered the know-how that helps readers walk that walk.

That's why a book on the essential skills of life was such a natural project for us. Let's face it, these days you can pay someone to do just about any task you need done. You can hire someone to trim your bushes, walk your dog, make your meals, and fix your car. And it's tempting, with all the entertaining gadgets available to us, to just plug in, zone out, and order everything you need online.

Tempting, but not really satisfying.

Real satisfaction comes from developing real skills. Ultimately, men worthy of the title can take care of themselves, their castle, their chariot, and the many big and small emergencies the world throws at them. Self-sufficiency may well be headed toward "lost art" status, but not among PM readers (or editors). We all realize that there are big rewards to knowing how to roll up your sleeves and attack what needs doing.

This book gives you the information to do just that. You'll discover that having that information at your fingertips is its own reward. There's something deeply satisfying about knowing you will be able to rise to the challenge, whether the task is fixing a leaking faucet, building a campfire from scratch, or performing CPR on a heart attack victim. Peace of mind comes from knowing that you're a well-rounded individual who's ready for whatever life has in store.

Of course, there are the more tangible rewards, like saving money on a home improvement project (or saving a life in the heat of the moment).

But whatever particular benefits you might derive from being today's "renaissance" man, the journey to self-sufficiency starts here. We've chosen those basic skills that touch on all segments of life. We cover the fundamentals of keeping your home, vehicle, and possessions in good working order. But we also provide insight on handling yourself in the great outdoors, where your skill set can make the difference between a relaxing nature vacation and a hellish survival nightmare. One of the most important sections we've included is the chapter on emergencies. You may only come across a choking victim once in your life, but your comprehension of Skill #8 could mean the difference between life or death for the guy who inhaled an overlarge piece of steak.

Lastly, no primer on skills would be complete without a cross-section of topics covering our coveted digital devices, from home theater systems to laptops and beyond.

The idea is to become the Swiss Army knife of men—not necessarily the perfect expert for every task, but certainly handy in almost any situation. That's the driving spirit behind the magazine and the ultimate goal of this book.    —The Editors of *Popular Mechanics*

# MISTER 911

The most crucial skill any man can have is how to react in any given emergency situation. Let's face it, it's easy to choke under pressure, and easier still to be just a hapless bystander when a car filled with a family of four goes into the water, or the boat you're in gets waylaid by rough seas. But if you're reading this book, that's not the type of man you want to be.

Mister 911 is the man who equips himself for emergencies first and foremost. Yeah, you know how to paint a room, change a tire, and tie the perfect knot, but it's especially important to you to be Johnny-on-the-spot when lives are at stake.

We've focused on emergency events that you're statistically most likely to come across at least once in your lifetime. Each entry gives you the simplest explanation of how to handle the situation. We know you're not a doctor, but you don't need to be one to stop a wound from bleeding or treat frostbite. Taking the appropriate action in a timely fashion can be as valuable as professional medical attention when the need arises.

So read on and hone your emergency-response skills. You never know when you'll need them.

# 1 · STOP A WOUND FROM BLEEDING

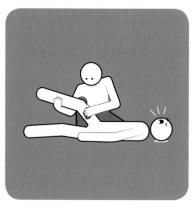

Your body was carefully designed to keep blood in. A wound ruins that ideal, so stopping the bleeding is the first order of business. Art Hsieh, chief operating officer and education director of the San Francisco Paramedic Association, knows better than most the value of keeping blood in. "There is a saying that 'every drop counts,' meaning every blood cell is precious. Blood is essential for moving oxygen and nutrients to cells, so it's wise to try to stop bleeding as quickly as possible."

The answer to stopping bleeding is, in a word, pressure. What you use to apply the pressure is less important than the pressure itself. As Hsieh explains, "It doesn't matter what you use really; the wound is probably contaminated the moment it was created. If you can, use something clean. But frankly, in cases of severe bleeding, the palm of your hand will work just fine." Of course, ideally, you should use latex gloves if possible and apply clean gauze to the wound. The idea is not only to keep any additional contamination out of the wound, but to keep blood from coming in contact with you.

Stopping blood flow isn't a fine art. Hsieh recommends using as much pressure as necessary to stop the bleeding, increasing the pressure if the blood flow doesn't slow down within a few seconds. If you're worried about catching anything from contact with the blood, realize that the potential for infection is very minor as long as you have no obvious cuts of your own on your hands. Hsieh adds, "As soon as you can, wash off the blood and any other bodily fluids with soap and water—that will reduce the chance of infection even further."

Lastly, Hsieh offers this for situations where you're still having trouble staunching the flow: "If you're not getting the bleeding under control with direct pressure, elevate the body part above the level of the heart. These two combined steps will probably manage nearly all types of bleeding." Of course, in very rare cases, true tourniquets may be needed." (See Skill #13: Apply a Tourniquet, page 34.)

TIP: If there is severe external bleeding or if you suspect internal bleeding, ask a bystander to call EMS while you attempt to staunch the flow. And, despite countless cinematic depictions of bullets being yanked out of wounds, do NOT probe a wound to remove a bullet or any other embedded object. Your priority is to stop the bleeding; leave the object in place.

# 2 · TREAT AN ANKLE SPRAIN

You don't have to be an athlete to be familiar with the pain of an ankle sprain. One moment you're walking off the curb, the next you're hopping along in pain. Most likely you're the victim of the ankle "roll" or "inversion" sprain (by far the most common type), in which the foot rolls to the outside as the ankle flexes inward. But call it what you will, it's simply painful.

The pain is caused by stretched or torn ligaments. The first (excuse the pun) step is to make sure you really are dealing with a sprain and not a more serious fracture. This, according to Dr. Yolanda Tun-Chiong, DO, of Sports Medicine at Chelsea in New York City, is a matter of some simple tests. "Immediately following the injury, if you can't put any weight on the foot at all, you need to get it X-rayed. Another test for possible fracture is point tenderness. If you touch the ankle bone on the inside or outside and there is sensitivity, or if there is a point of sensitivity on either side of the bottom midpoint of the foot (base of the fifth toe), you need to take a trip to the ER."

If, on the other hand, you're just limping and sore, take Dr. Tun-Chiong's advice and apply RICE. "RICE stands for Rest, Ice, Compression, and Elevation. The idea is to use all of these to reduce pain and swelling. Ice the ankle for 20 minutes every couple of hours and keep it elevated as much as possible."

And wrap the ankle for two reasons—to compress and contain swelling, and to stabilize the joint from further damage. Dr. Tun-Chiong says, "When you first injure the ankle, you'll want to wrap it with something stiff to stop the ankle from moving, such as an ankle brace. A simple compression wrap applied with the foot in an L and securely covering the mid-foot area up to the high ankle will keep swelling down during normal activities."

First loop the compression wrap once around the instep, then up and once around the ankle (1). Next wrap it across the top and bottom of the ankle in a figure eight, making sure the wrap is tight, but not so tight that it is cutting circulation (2). Finish by circling the high ankle, then clipping the wrap to secure it (3).

TIP: Not everybody has ice or an ice pack on hand—especially if you don't have an icemaker. Dr. Tun-Chiong suggests, "Take out frozen vegetables or meat and press it on your ankle." Do not apply ice or a frozen substance directly to the skin. Cover the area with a thin, clean cloth before applying.

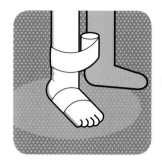

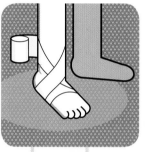

# 3 · SPLINT A BROKEN BONE

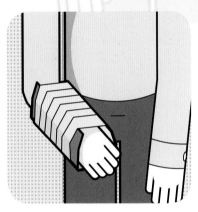

The human body contains a lot of opportunities for broken bones. But the goal of splinting any break is the same: immobilize the bone to prevent further injury.

The signs of a break may be subtle or obvious. In the case of a serious fracture, the victim may experience a grinding sensation when the bone is moved, or the end of the broken bone may have pierced the skin (avert your eyes if necessary). More commonly, signs of a fracture include swelling and bruising, point tenderness, and the inability to bear weight. If you suspect there's a fracture, you should use a splint to stabilize the area until you can consult a medical professional.

Dr. Clifford Stark, DO, medical director of Sports Medicine at Chelsea in New York City and director of sports medicine and orthopedics at Columbia University Family Medicine Residency, says of the process, "Splinting is limited only by the materials available and imagination. Basically, you need to splint through the joint above and below the suspected fracture. The splint should be secure and tight, but not so much as to constrict the blood flow (fingers or toes shouldn't turn blue). Position the splint to make it as comfortable as possible for the patient."

You can use the traditional sticks or long pieces of wood and torn ribbons of fabric, but Dr. Stark suggests a more commonplace solution, shown opposite. "Cardboard is probably the most effective commonly available material with which to build a splint. It needs to run the length of the bone past the joints on either end. The cardboard can be bent around to cover most of the skin around the extremity and should be wrapped with an elastic wrap. ACE bandages are probably best but certain athletic-type tapes can suffice as well."

Dr. Stark stresses that all suspected fractures should receive prompt medical attention. But he adds, "Displaced fractures, open fractures (bone poking through skin), and those where blood flow to an extremity is affected require emergency medical care."

**TIP: According to Dr. Stark, you can use a "poor man's test" to determine a fracture. Hold a tuning fork against the tender area. If the vibration significantly increases the degree of tenderness, it is most likely a fracture.**

# 4 · TREAT A BAD BURN

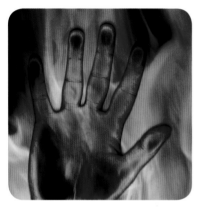

We all learned as children not to touch a hot stove. Unfortunately, many of us don't extend that learning to open pilot flames, exhaust manifolds, and long summer days at the beach. But prolonged exposure to any heat source can result in burns that require medical attention, which is why the first step to take in treating a burn is to get away from the source, whether it's a hot surface, burning liquid or steam, or the sun. If your clothes are on fire, remove them immediately. If that's not possible without further injury, remember that other childhood gem and stop, drop, and roll.

The next step, according to Dr. James Jeng, associate director of the Burn Center at Washington Hospital Center in Washington, D. C., is to assess the severity of the burn. "A first-degree burn involves only the top layer of skin with no blistering—the burn is red and pink and skin doesn't fluff off." For this, Dr. Jeng recommends, "You need to replenish fluids carefully and avoid getting dehydrated. Advil is pretty much magic medicine for this type of burn, but make sure you're not dehydrated, because if you are, Advil can pickle your kidneys." He adds, "Running cold water over the burn can relieve some of the pain."

Second- and third-degree burns require medical attention—even if you don't think the burn is severe. As Dr. Jeng explains, "Second-degree burns need medical attention either immediately or eventually, depending on the size of the burn. The burn site blisters, is wet and painful to the touch. First aid is basically soap and water and then just a dry sterile dressing, after which you should get yourself to the hospital or your doctor. The medical treatment is going to involve antibiotic cream and may focus on preventing scarring."

Dr. Jeng emphasizes quick treatment for the worst burns. "Third-degree burns are where the whole thickness of the skin has been killed or burned away. These uniformly require operations, and need medical treatment as promptly as possible. The hallmark of a third-degree burn is that it is no longer painful because even the nerve fibers in the skin have been killed by the heat."

# 5 · DEAL WITH AN ALLERGIC REACTION TO A STING

Proving that dynamite comes in small packages, tiny stinging insects can pack a potentially deadly punch. In fact, some people die from anaphylactic reactions to stings. The trick to keeping yourself and others out of that unfortunate group is knowing the difference between normal reactions and the systemic reactions that can quickly snowball into serious problems.

The vast majority of stings result in normal pain and localized swelling, according to Dr. David Golden of Johns Hopkins Hospital in Baltimore, Maryland. "Some people, because they have sensitive skin, may get bigger than average swellings, something the size of a golf ball or an egg."

If you're allergic to the sting of a yellow jacket, honeybee, wasp, or hornet, you may experience a conspicuous swelling. Dr. Golden says, "These may take more than a day to develop and can last for 5 to 10 days and may be up to 8 inches or more. You may be stung in your finger and a day later end up being swollen up to your shoulder." Although this type of reaction often prompts a visit to the emergency room, Dr. Golden suggests using your judgment. "If it's not too big, just use ice packs, cold compresses, antihistamines, and pain relievers. But there's nothing dangerous about even a large local swelling unless it happens to be in your tongue or throat."

The greatest cause for concern is a reaction away from the site of the sting. Dr. Golden explains, "A systemic reaction, or 'anaphylaxis,' is when you get stung on your toe and your throat swells or you get hives all over. Systemic reactions usually involve hives, throat swelling, or dizziness, or some combination of the three. And that is potentially dangerous and potentially life threatening." A systemic reaction should lead you to the doors of the nearest emergency room, where more than likely they will give you a shot of epinephrine. Dr. Golden says, "Fatal reactions to stings are almost always the result of not getting an epinephrine injection in a timely fashion. That's the only antidote."

**TIP: If you suspect that you might be allergic or have had a reaction to a sting, discuss it with your doctor or allergist. They may want you to carry an "epi-pen," a portable epinephrine injector. It's also not a bad idea to include one in the emergency kit you take along when backpacking or camping in the wilderness.**

# 6 · COPE WITH FOOD POISONING

Eating is one of those great joys in life until you consume potato salad that's been left out in the sun too long. Whether food poisoning comes from the common *Staph* or *Salmonella* bacteria that results from poor food hygiene, or is the product of potent botulism toxins in homemade salsa your mom canned last year, the symptoms are largely the same: vomiting, diarrhea, abdominal cramping, and a heartfelt desire to be taken out of your misery.

Don't despair, says Dr. Tom Arnold, medical director for the Louisiana Poison Control Center, chances are you're not going to die even if it feels like it for a short while. In most cases, you won't need to seek medical attention but you do need to give your system a break. "First, let your stomach rest for a while; don't take anything by mouth for a few hours until your stomach's had a chance to settle down," Dr. Arnold counsels. "Start intake again with clear liquids such as water or sports drinks." Vomiting and diarrhea lead to dehydration and loss of mineral salts; water and sports drinks will help replenish your supplies.

The rest is about slowly returning to a normal diet. Dr. Arnold suggests, "Start with a 'BRAT' diet—Bananas, Rice, Applesauce, and Toast. These are easy on the stomach and digest simply and quickly. As you start to feel better and get your appetite back, add in normal foods."

However, you should be prepared for several days of discomfort. Along the way, if you experience bloody vomit or diarrhea, or neurological symptoms such as muscle weakness, seizures, or a high fever, or if symptoms persist for more than a week, get yourself medical care without delay.

# 7 · TAKE THE NIP OUT OF FROSTBITE

Cold, oh so cold. If you're an avid skier, mountain climber, or all-around winter enthusiast, you know how it feels when the mercury drops into the single digits, and the wind chill makes it feel even colder.

That kind of cold can lead to frostbite, a serious risk if you're fond of your fingers and toes.

Garrett Madison, expedition manager for Alpine Ascents, has seen more than his share of frostbite among mountain climbers. He stresses that the first line of defense in treating frostbite is recognizing it. "The first stage is 'frost nip,' with a pins-and-needles sensation in the skin, and the skin is white and soft. With superficial frostbite the skin has a waxy, frozen feeling and is numb. In deep frostbite, blood vessels, nerves, tendons, bones, and muscles might all be frozen with permanent damage. This presents a risk of gangrene (blackened tissue that died after blood vessels froze) and blood clots in really severe cases." He adds, "People with deep frostbite often lose toes or fingers that have been affected."

The key to limiting frostbite damage is, quite simply, getting warm. As soon as you notice any sign of frostbite, such as a pain in an exposed area of skin, or numbness in extremities, get inside and get warm. Madison advises a gradual rewarming. "Rewarm slowly by putting on dry warm clothes or by exposing affected areas to warm air, or a warm object. Any sudden and severe change in temperature is always difficult for a body to absorb." Sucking down a warm drink such as tea will help as well. Do not rub frostbitten skin or, despite what you've seen in the movies, rub snow on it. Rewarming may be accompanied by a burning sensation; take a pain reliever such as aspirin or ibuprofen to lessen the discomfort.

If you have frost nip but the feeling returns quickly to the affected area and skin is pink again, the area is thawed. However, according to Madison, if you show signs of even superficial frostbite, you should seek medical attention to limit the possibility of permanent damage. Exposure to cold also puts you in danger of hypothermia, a condition in which your body's internal temperature drops below normal. (See Skill #12: Reversing Hypothermia, page 32).

**TIP: If you're planning on partying, stay indoors in cold weather. As Madison cautions, "Limit the use of alcohol or tobacco because those drugs can impede the circulation to your extremities, increasing the possibility and severity of frostbite."**

# 8 · STOP SOMEONE FROM CHOKING

With all the press it gets, you could be forgiven for thinking the Heimlich maneuver is the cure-all for anyone choking. Not so, says Dr. David Markenson, chief of pediatric emergency medicine at the Maria Fareri Children's Hospital at Westchester County Medical Center in New York and chair of the American Red Cross Advisory Council on First Aid, Aquatics, Safety, and Preparedness.

According to Dr. Markenson, the famous maneuver is just one step in a more involved process. "If someone appears to be choking, first approach him from the front and decide if he is truly choking. If the person can cough or speak, the airway is not completely blocked and he can still remove the object on his own. In that case, just watch the person to make sure the object clears."

Call 911 so that an ambulance is there if the situation worsens. And keep the person in sight. Dr. Markenson points out, "Often people are embarrassed when choking so they try to get out of sight, into a bathroom for instance. Unfortunately, there are many cases where those people die because there's nobody around to help them."

If it becomes clear the person's airway is blocked—basically, if he isn't making any noise—it's time to swing into action. "First, position yourself beside and slightly behind the person and do five back blows," says Dr. Markenson. "Use the heel of your hand to strike the person between the shoulder blades after helping him to lean slightly forward, and continue to help him stay balanced and standing (1). That will usually clear the blockage."

If back blows don't do the trick, it's time for the next step. As Dr. Markenson describes it, "If the blockage isn't cleared, go to the abdominal thrust, also known as the Heimlich maneuver." Move behind the person, place your arms around the person's waist, and

clasp your hands just above the belly button (the hand touching the person is a fist, with the thumb side toward the person's belly), and thrust upward into the chest cavity five times, or until the object becomes dislodged (2). The combination of back blows and abdominal thrusts will normally clear the blockage. But Dr. Markenson adds, "Sometimes this doesn't work. If the airway isn't cleared, unfortunately over time the victim will become unconscious. Lower them to the ground, and transition to plain old CPR (see Skill #9, opposite). Do a combination of 30 chest thrusts, and then attempt to blow in their mouth to detect if the object is cleared." Continue until the object clears or emergency medical personnel take over.

In some cases, you'll need to adjust your technique. As Dr. Markenson explains, "With an obese or pregnant person you won't be able to get your hands around their abdomen for the abdominal thrusts. Instead, position your hands between their nipples, and thrust there. With a choking child, you need to either get down to their level so that you're thrusting rather than lifting the child up, or sit the child on your lap."

**TIP: To help a choking infant—a child younger than one year old—support him face down on your forearm, so that his head is held in your palm beneath the level of his chest, with his mouth uncovered. Use the heel of your free hand to give the baby five firm slaps between his shoulder blades. If this doesn't clear the airway, turn the baby over, and give him five quick firm thrusts on the sternum, using three fingers. If you can see something in the baby's mouth remove it; if the baby is not breathing, call 911 and begin CPR. If the airway blockage does not come out, continue with back slaps and chest thrusts until the object comes out or paramedics arrive.**

# 9 · PERFORM CPR

. . . . . . . . . . . . . . . . . . . . . . . . . . . . . . . . . . . . . . . . . . . . . .

Most people have an idea of how to perform cardio-pulmonary resuscitation (CPR), but you may not have taken a course in years. Here's a refresher that will help you prolong signs of life until medics arrive.

Phone for medical help, then look and listen for the victim's breathing. Open the airway by tilting the head back and lifting the chin so that the teeth almost touch.

Pinch both nostrils closed; bend over his face and fully cover his mouth with yours (1). Give two full rescue breaths, making sure to breathe deeply.

Place your dominant hand on the middle of the victim's chest (2). Put your other hand on top and interlock your fingers. Straighten your arms and begin compressing the chest $1\frac{1}{2}$ to 2 inches with the heels of your hands (3). Continue the compression/breathing cycle, compressing 30 times and then breathing twice, until the person starts breathing or help arrives.

TIP: Remember a baby's lungs are much smaller than yours: to perform CPR on an infant younger than one year old, give two gentle rescue breaths, each one lasting just one second. Use only the pads of two or three fingers, just below an imaginary line running between the babies nipples, to compress the chest 30 times at the rate of 100 compressions per minute. Continue alternating rescue breaths and compressions until the baby revives or help arrives.

. . . . . . . . . . . . . . . . . . . . . . . . . . . . . . . . . . . . . . . . . . . . . .

# 11 · TREAT SOMEONE IN SHOCK FROM AN INJURY

Give props to your body for always trying to do the right thing for your health, no matter what the circumstance. When that circumstance is an injury, the action your body takes is called shock.

"Shock is basically a lack of blood supply to the organs," says Dr. L. Keith Scott, associate professor of medicine, pediatrics, and surgery at Louisiana State University. "It's your body's way of preserving critical functions like breathing, by sacrificing less critical functions like keeping extremities warm."

Which is why the hallmark sign of shock is a cold and clammy body. Paramedics are trained to use sight and touch as first indicators of shock and you can, too. If an accident victim looks and feels cold and clammy, assume they're in shock.

From there, Dr. Scott advises, "The most important thing is not to do additional harm. So, for instance, if the person has been in a car wreck, immobilize them. If there is bleeding, stop the bleeding with direct pressure (see Skill #1: Stop a Wound from Bleeding, page 10). Don't try to correct any other problems, just immobilize and stop the bleeding. The body will adapt to low blood pressure and low oxygen, given time, and people will recover from that very well. But victims often die on the street because their bleeding wasn't stopped." Because a shock victim's condition can deteriorate quickly, monitor the person's "ABC's" (airway, breathing, and circulation or pulse) and, if the victim stops breathing, begin CPR (see Skill #9: Perform CPR, page 27) or take other lifesaving measures as necessary.

Lastly, Dr. Scott emphasizes that you shouldn't try to warm up the shock victim. "The data is very clear right now that the body goes cold and clammy for a reason. So keep the victim cold. The body knows what to do; for the most part, we just have to get out of its way."

# 18 · BREAK FREE FROM A RIP CURRENT

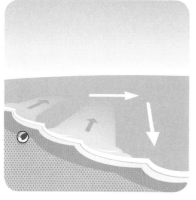

The ocean flexes its muscles in many ways, but one of the most disconcerting is the rip current.

Mistakenly called a "riptide" (there's no tide involved) or "undertow" (it doesn't pull you under), the rip current is a common ocean phenomenon that can be easily survived if you are a good swimmer, according to B.J. Fisher, health and safety director for the American Lifeguard Association. The trick—as with so many emergencies—is to not panic and keep your wits about you.

A rip current occurs when the normal action of waves being pushed along the shore by the wind is interrupted by a low point or break in the sandbar. The water hits the depression and rushes back out to sea. As Fisher describes, "These are strong currents that can pull even an experienced swimmer away from shore. Drowning usually results from panic and fatigue. An estimated 80 percent of ocean saves performed by lifeguards are related to rip currents."

The thing to keep in mind, Fisher says, is that even though rip currents can run out well over a hundred yards off shore, they are generally no wider than 100 feet. "Depending on where you are, even if you're in the very center of a rip current, you only have 30 to 50 feet to swim out of it." And that's the secret to beating the rip current: simply swim your way out of it.

As Fisher says, "The mistake is to fight it. Remain calm to conserve energy and think clearly. Swim out of the current by swimming parallel to the shoreline. When you're out of the current—and you'll feel it because a rip current can move up to 8 mph—swim toward shore."

Of course, as a lifeguard himself, Fisher realizes that some novice swimmers may have trouble making it out of the current. He advises, "If you are unable to swim out of the rip current, float or calmly tread water. Once you are out of the current, swim toward the shore. If you are still unable to reach shore, draw attention to yourself by waving your arms and yelling for help."

# 19 · PUT OUT A FIRE WITH AN EXTINGUISHER

Even a small household fire can quickly grow out of control. That's why preparation is key, and the first step is to make sure you have the right fire extinguisher for the job and understand how to use it. The three extinguisher ratings for household use are A (ordinary combustibles such as wood and paper), B (flammable liquids), and C (electrical). But a dry-chemical "ABC" extinguisher is usually your best bet, because it will put out just about any fire you're likely to encounter in the home.

As for dealing with the fire itself, Ryan O'Donnell, chief executive officer of BullEx Digital Safety in Troy, New York, suggests learning the handy acronym APASS, which stands for Alert, Pull, Aim, Squeeze, Sweep. "Alert means first call for help. If the fire is large enough to fight with an extinguisher, you're still going to want the fire department to respond. Even if you get the fire out, they can check for fire spread behind walls and other unseen areas."

O'Donnell also cautions against fighting a fire when fleeing is a better idea. "In basic terms, if a fire is taller than you, it has progressed beyond the incipient stage and is too large to fight with an extinguisher. When faced with a fire of this size, if the room is filled with smoke, or if your instincts tell you to evacuate, evacuate immediately."

If the fire is small enough, follow the rest of the acronym, as O'Donnell describes:

1. *Pull* the pin in the handle. This often means breaking the tamper seal. On most extinguishers, twisting the pin and then pulling it out helps to break the tamper seal, allowing the pin to be removed with less force.

2. *Aim* the nozzle at the base of the fire (but don't squeeze the trigger yet). Hold the extinguisher by its handle with one hand and use the other hand to establish your aim.

3. *Squeeze* the trigger once the nozzle is steady and aimed at the fire's base. This discharges the pressurized dry chemical.

4. *Sweep* in a controlled motion that directs the spray from one side of the fire's base to the other. Aim only at the base of the fire because hitting the flames won't do much to extinguish it.

Lastly, O'Donnell stresses, "Don't ever turn your back on any fire. Once the fire is extinguished, back away slowly. When the fire department arrives they will conduct a thorough investigation to check for any smoldering 'hot spots' or hidden fire."

# 20 · ESCAPE A BURNING BUILDING

On average, between four and eight people lose their lives in a fire every day. However, many of those deaths could have been prevented with a modest amount of planning and knowledge of some simple evacuation techniques.

Planning is the first step, according to Captain Dave Winkler, specialized instructor for the El Camino Fire Academy in Inglewood, California. "The quicker you know about a fire, the better chance you have of getting out. Install smoke detectors—especially in locations such as garages, basements, and attics where a fire can quickly grow undetected."

Winkler also suggests creating an escape plan for your home and practicing it. If you're staying in a hotel, review the posted escape routes and come up with an escape plan. Any plan should account for the needs of children, elderly, or disabled members of the family, and everyone in the household should know the plan.

But preparation doesn't stop at the evacuation plan. Winkler advises, "Make sure your windows open easily and are not painted shut. Equip upper floors with escape ladders and be sure that window bars have approved releases and open easily."

The rest, as Winkler points out, is a matter of following the prescribed route of escape. "When you hear an alarm or detect a fire, immediately exit using your primary escape route—the route you normally use to go in and out. Along the way, feel any closed door you need to go through with the back of your hand. If it is warm to the touch, open it slowly to investigate and find another way out if fire is on the other side."

He adds, "Move quickly and conserve energy. If it's smoky, cover your mouth with material or cloth and stay as low as possible; the coolest and freshest air will be down low. Close doors behind you to slow the progress of the fire." If you're in an unfamiliar building, try to stay oriented as you exit. If you become turned around, follow a wall, always moving in the same direction. This will ensure you don't waste precious time and energy going in circles. And, of course, never use an elevator to exit.

TIP: Winkler suggests that when vacationing in a multistory hotel, book a room below the seventh floor. Most fire department aerial devices will only reach the seventh floor, though the max might be lower if there are obstacles at the base of the building.

# 21 · REPLACE A PANE OF GLASS

"The first thing to know is that if you've got a double-pane window you need a pro," says Douglas Sanders, an owner, along with his father, of the 100-year-old Millen Hardware in Wilmette, Illinois. "Because that means it's either vacuum sealed or there's a gas in there for insulation. So these instructions are for fixing a single-pane window."

Step one is to remove the wood molding or the glazing putty (1). "If you're dealing with a broken window it's safer to knock all the glass out first and then clean it up," Sanders says. "Wear goggles and really thick gloves, and be careful not to cut yourself."

Use a pry bar to remove molding, or a putty knife to cut away the putty. "It can be a lot of labor if the putty is not softened," Sanders says. "One trick is to use a hair dryer to heat and soften it." When you've removed your molding/putty, you'll see several clips holding the window in place. "Imagine the back of a picture frame, with those clips used to hold the picture in place," Sanders says. "Those clips are called 'glazing points.' Pull them out with needle-nose pliers and remove the rest of the glass."

Here's the critical point. "Measure the glass space and subtract $1/8$ inch," Sanders says, "because window frames are never square—temperature changes, house settling, and so on—so you'll need the play." Now replace the glass and new glazing points, and then reattach the molding or apply new glazing putty (2).

"Basically, what you are doing with the putty is making a molding," Sanders says. "Fill up the ledge, and make a smooth transition between the frame and the window. Let it dry two weeks and paint."

# 22 · RECAULK A TUB

· · · · · · · · · · · · · · · · · · · · · · · · · · · · · · · · · · · · · · · · · · · · · · · · · ·

Even the best caulk has a limited lifespan, so when the mold overpowers your tub's edge seal, lay down a new bead. (This process also works for brand-new tubs).

1. The first step is to soften the existing caulk with a **caulk remover.**
2. Next, slice through the softened caulk with a **utility knife,** fitted with a new blade. If you're lucky, most of it will fall free. On the other hand, if there are several layers or if the caulk is very thick, you may need to pull the remaining material from the joint with a pair of **needle-nose pliers.**
3. Rake remaining chunks of caulk from the joint using the hook end of a painter's **five-in-one tool.**
4. The final preparation step is to clean the surface and remove mildew. Use a non-ammoniated bath cleaner to remove soap scum. Do not use an ammoniated cleaner prior to applying bleach because, when mixed together, they give off poisonous fumes. Kill any mildew on the surfaces using a solution of $1/3$ cup bleach to 1 gallon of water. Use a paintbrush or **foam brush** to apply the solution and to work it into the gap left by the removed caulk. Scrub the area with a brush or plastic pad, rinse, then dry the surfaces with a clean rag.
5. Finally, use a **caulk gun** to apply a bead of tub-and-tile caulk containing a fungicide around the edge of the tub. Smooth the bead of the caulk with a wet fingertip and let it set overnight before showering or bathing.

· · · · · · · · · · · · · · · · · · · · · · · · · · · · · · · · · · · · · · · · · · · · · · · · · ·

STEP
1

STEP
2

STEP
3

STEP
4

STEP
5

# 23 · REPLACE A CRACKED CERAMIC TILE

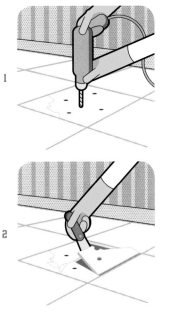

If you're a little clumsy with your favorite cast-iron pan, you'll find out just how surprisingly fragile ceramic floor tiles really are. Fortunately, replacing a tile—even in the middle of a floor—is a fairly easy task.

First, remove the damaged tile. Danny Lipford, home repair expert and host of the TV show *Today's Homeowner,* suggests using a masonry bit to drill a number of holes in the center of the tile (1) so that you can begin to chip out the tile (2). "Use a brick chisel and hammer to just chip out the tile, but remember to wear safety glasses. Those little ceramic slivers can be nasty."

As you remove the tile, use an adhesive remover to clean the subfloor of any adhesive. "Use a putty knife to remove the adhesive and tile, so that the surface is nice and smooth for the new tile," says Lipford. "Just be careful in removing the grout around the edges, so that you don't damage the surrounding tile."

After all the old tile, adhesive, and grout is removed, you're ready to set in the new tile. Lipford recommends using a tile saved from when the floor was initially laid. If you neglected to set aside any of the original tile, match a new tile as closely as possible to the color of the existing floor. Lipford says, "Use a thin-set adhesive applied evenly with a notched trowel to avoid hollow spots underneath the tile (3). Grout around the tile the next day with a grout that matches the rest of the floor (4). Pay particular attention to how the other grout was applied, whether it was laid flush with the surface of the tile, or rubbed down to a little concave around the tile. There again, match the grout color as closely as possible."

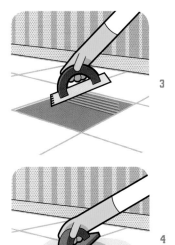

**TIP:** Even if you're working from the original bag of grout, it may not match perfectly. That's why Lipford suggests one last step. "Go ahead and put that grout down, let it dry for a few weeks. If you're just not happy with how it blends in, use a grout stain on the whole floor to create a consistent look. Grout stain is inexpensive and easy to apply, and it's just amazing how it blends everything in."

# 24 · REPAIR A HOLE IN DRYWALL

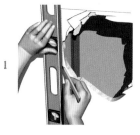

It only takes one quick game of indoor football to punch a hole in your drywall that no picture can cover up. Now it's time for post-game repair.

1. Draw a square around the hole. Use a level to center one side of the square on a nearby stud.

2. Cut three sides of the square using a drywall saw. Remove the drywall over the stud using a utility knife.

3. Next, use a piece of 1" x 4" pine to provide backing for the repair panel. Apply a generous amount of construction adhesive to the backing board. Fasten the backing board to the surrounding drywall with clamps.

4. After the adhesive has dried, cut a repair panel to fit, and fasten it to the stud and the backing board with drywall screws.

5. Apply self-adhering fiberglass mesh tape over the repair-panel seams. Overlap the tape at the corners for maximum strength, and center each piece over a seam.

6. Use a 3- or 4-in. drywall knife to apply the first layer of drywall compound over the tape. Smooth the dried compound with a hand sander and coarse sanding mesh. Level the repair with the surrounding surface and apply several skim coats of drywall compound over the repaired area. Use an 8-in. taping knife and sand only the last coat.

# 25 · FIX POPPING NAILS AND SCREWS

It's a sad fact of construction that wood shrinks and buildings shift. That's why unsightly nail or screw pops are commonplace in drywall.

1. First, twist a utility knife into the area around the popped fastener to remove the joint compound from around it. Then, use a nail set to sink the nail back below the surface of the drywall, or screw in a popped screw.

2. Next, drive drywall screws in above and below to ensure that the fastener doesn't pop again.

3. Finally, cover the nail and screw heads with joint compound, let it dry, then sand and repaint the wall.

# 26 · PAINT A ROOM

Good paint jobs start before the first can of paint is opened.

Prepare the room by removing all hardware (door latch sets, receptacle and switch plates). Don't just fill small holes in the plaster or drywall; enlarge them first so the compound can be pushed in place. Sand rough spots, wash dirty areas, then prime.

Paint the ceiling, then the walls. Use a $2^1/_2$-in. brush to cut in the finish color at all corners and against the trim. Switch to a roller, apply paint in a W-shape pattern, and fill it in (1). After you dip the roller in the paint tray, 70 percent of the paint comes off on the first downstroke; avoid splatters by starting at least 9 inches from the corner. Apply two coats.

Finish by painting the woodwork and trim with a gloss or semigloss paint (2). It's safest to mask off the walls beforehand, although pros often skip this step. If you do mask, use a tape designed for the purpose so the adhesive doesn't pull the paint from the wall. Once the final coat dries, reinstall the hardware and get back to life as normal.

# 27 · MOVE HEAVY STUFF

Whether it's a washing machine or an antique dresser, moving bulky, weighty household furnishings or appliances is no picnic. Doing it the right way can be the difference between a quick and painless chore and a herniated disk.

Chris Wells, owner-operator of A-Mrazek Moving Systems, Inc., a United Van Lines affiliate, is all too aware of how moving heavy objects can take a toll. That's why he stresses simple solutions that rely more on physics than elbow grease. "If you're just moving something from one room to another by yourself, use a blanket. Tilt one end up and bunch the blanket underneath, then tilt the other end up and pull the blanket through, so that the washing machine, or whatever it is, is sitting on the blanket. Then it's easy to just pull it to wherever you want it to go."

Even though he favors brains over brawn, Wells is quick to point out the value of a partner. "If you're moving something like a refrigerator or dresser up or down stairs, use a nylon strap. Run it under the item, and have the downstairs-side person hoist the strap to chest level. Then the upstairs person does the same, and you can lift the piece without bending over and risking a back injury."

Of course, sometimes friends are a rare commodity on moving day. If you find you absolutely have to take something up or down stairs by yourself, you can use what Wells describes as "the slide method." "Unfold a large cardboard box, like the ones used for refrigerators, and make a slide on top of the stairs. Lay whatever you're moving on its side, and slide it down, or guide and pull it up."

But Wells cautions that you should be extremely careful not to put yourself in a position where the item could fall or slip on top of you (that's why he advises to pull, rather than push, it up the stairs). "Really, the easiest way to move something large, whether you're by yourself or not, is the refrigerator dolly," he concludes. "They're inexpensive to rent, simple to use, and they make moving heavy pieces easy."

# 28 · FIX A STICKING DOOR

A sticking door is a small but persistent irritant. Happily, ridding yourself of this particular nagging problem is a matter of making some simple adjustments to how the door is mounted.

First, check the hinges to make sure that they are not loose; tighten any loose hinge screws. A sagging door can be the cause of stickiness. Next, check that the bottom hinge is not mortised too deeply. The mortise is the recess into which the hinge is set. If it is conspicuously deep compared to the hinge mortise above it, correct this by inserting a cardboard shim between the lower hinge leaf and the doorjamb. This will reposition the door so that it fits properly in its jamb.

If that doesn't solve the problem and the door binds just slightly, you may be able to insert a $3^1/2$-in.-long woodscrew to pull the upper part of the jamb toward the doorframe. To do this, remove the hinge leaf that is attached to the doorjamb. Next, bore three holes into the bottom of the hinge mortise. Start by boring a shallow saucer-shaped hole for the screw head, then bore a hole for the screw shank, and finally, make a third and smaller pilot hole for the screw's threaded portion.

You can bore these holes with three separate bits, or use a taper-point drill bit and then bore the countersunk hole for the screw head. To match the bits to the screw, simply hold the screw over each drill bit. The first hole should equal the head diameter, the next should be slightly larger than the shank, and the pilot hole should equal the screw's diameter minus the threads.

After you've driven the screw, reattach the hinge leaf to conceal the repair— and, voilà, your sticky little problem should be a thing of the past.

# 29 · REPLACE A TOILET TANK BALL

For most of us, the sound of a toilet tank running is a kind of water torture. Time to make the torture go away.

A tank leak will cause intermittent running as the toilet's fill valve briefly opens and admits water. The cause may be that the tank ball lands off-center on the flush valve. (Otherwise, it's the valve itself). The ball is the black wedge-shaped thing, not the big copper melon; that's the float.

Flush the toilet and check the ball's position on the valve. Adjust the lift-wire guide as needed (1). Next, run your figures over the ball. If your fingers come away slimy and black, replace the ball with a flapper valve.

To replace the ball, first turn the water off and drain the tank. Remove the old parts, then slide the flapper's mounting collar onto the overflow tube (2). Hook the flapper-valve wings over the collar's pegs (3). Say good-bye to water torture.

# 30 · FIX A LEAKY FAUCET

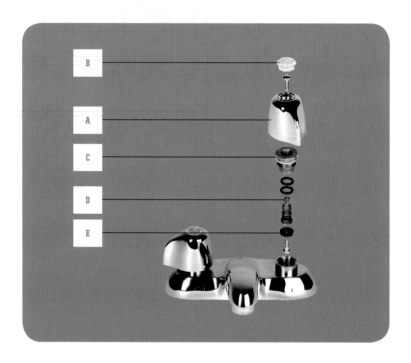

"First, you need to figure out what kind of faucet you have," says Douglas Sanders, the home-improvement guru at Millen Hardware in Wilmette, Illinois. "There are four basic types: a washer type with a washer resting on a metal seat (see illustration); a cartridge type which is usually a single-handle faucet with an O-ring instead of a washer; a ball type (with a metal or plastic ball resting on a rubber assembly) that tends to leak from the handle or housing; and a ceramic stem valve type—similar to cartridges.

The following fix-it rules refer to the common washer type, but the same general principles apply to all four types of faucet. And you always start by closing the supply valves under the sink. Step one: remove the handle (A). "There's not usually an exposed screw, but a screw cap (B) located in the center of the handle," says Sanders, who has helped hundreds of do-it-yourselfers navigate faucet repair. "Pry the cap off and then unscrew, being careful not to scratch anything."

You'll then see what's called a stem or "bonnet" nut (C). "They're usually hexagonal or square, and often made of soft steel so be careful not to strip it," Sanders says. "And sometimes they're recessed so you might need a socket wrench."

Pull the stem (D) out and you'll see a screw at the bottom of it: unscrew it and there's your washer (E). If you have a variety pack of washers, choose a replacement. Otherwise, take the assembly and washer to a hardware store to find a match, and grab some plumber's grease, too. Now, head back home and replace the washer.

"Put a little plumber's grease on the threads of the stem," Sanders says. "That will make it easier to turn your faucet on and off when you're finished, and easier to pull the stem out if you have to fix it again." Replace everything in reverse order, and break out your favorite water glass.

"A lot of people find their faucets still leak after replacing the washers," Sanders says. "Usually that means the old washer was worn so thin that metal was grinding against metal between stem and seat. If so, you'll need to replace the seat, or buy a 'seat-dressing tool.' They're used to grind the surfaces down, making them smooth so the washer can properly seal."

# 31 · FIX A CLOGGED KITCHEN DRAIN

There's nothing like a clogged kitchen sink to make you want to eat out. But depending on the clog, the solution may be easier than you think. First, think twice about dumping caustic drain cleaners down the drain. Many contain sulfuric acid or equally frightening chemical compounds—it only takes one splash back to ruin a day. So leave the chemical solutions as a last resort, and even then, opt for enzyme-based products (they work more slowly, but are less likely to hurt pipes).

If you live by the adage that there's nothing that doesn't taste better deep-fried, you'll inevitably clog the drain's arteries with a clot of grease from time to time. This simple heating-pad solution can clear that up. Wrap a heating pad around the drain trap until the metal becomes hot. This will melt the grease and you can flush it out with a running stream of hot water. If you don't have a heating pad, a hair dryer will do.

More likely, your clog will be composed of fibrous food material. In this case, first try a plunger. Fill the sink with water, cover the second drain if it's a double sink, and plunge away. The clog should break up fairly quickly. If it doesn't, it's time for plan C—the snake.

You can purchase an inexpensive hand snake at any home center or well-equipped hardware store. Run the snake down the drain until you meet the blockage, rotate it to cut through the clog, and pull what's left back up and out of the drain. You may not be able to reach the clog from the sink, in which case you'll need to take the extra step of removing the trap and trap arm, then snaking the drain line that comes out of the wall.

If you have a garbage disposal, skip right to the final snaking option because access to the clog will be blocked by the disposal itself.

Save yourself any further drainage frustrations with a weekly ritual of pouring a couple taps from a box of baking soda down the drain, followed by a rinse of boiling water.

# 32 · FLUSH A HOT WATER HEATER

Heating all the hot water for a house can be awfully dirty business, which is why sediment periodically collects in your water heater. Signs that sediment buildup has reached critical mass in a gas-fired appliance include knocking and rumbling. Excess sediment not only decreases heating efficiency (meaning bigger energy bills), it can even reduce the life of a water heater. A simple flush can have a big impact.

Turn the heater's gas control to the "Pilot" setting. Then shut off the cold-water supply to the heater and attach a hose to the tank's drain valve. Open a hot-water faucet at a nearby sink to prevent a vacuum from forming in the heater, and open the heater's drain valve. The water flowing out of the hose will be murky at first. When it runs clear, shut the valve.

When the job is done, you'll probably find that the water heater's drain valve will not shut completely because it's partially blocked by corrosion and sediment. Be prepared: buy a hose cap and tightly screw it onto the valve. If you can't find a cap with an internal gasket, buy Teflon plumbing tape and apply it to the valve threads before tightening the cap. To refill the heater, open the cold-water supply while leaving the hot-water faucet open. When water flows freely from the faucet, close it and return the gas control to the "On" setting.

# 33 · FIX A DEAD OUTLET

If the lamp goes out, but the bulb's not fried, it's time to check the outlet. Once you turn off the breaker and remove the cover plate, here's how to fix the usual culprits.

**Detached wire:** Cut the damaged wire $1/8$ inch from the end and strip $1/2$ inch of the insulation. Reattach by loosening the terminal screw a couple of turns, then bend the wire clockwise beneath it and tighten the screw.

**Loose push-in connection:** Reattach the loose wire on the back of the outlet under the terminal screw with the broken connection.

**Loose splice:** Remove the wire connector (aka wire nut) and replace it with a new wire connector. Hold the stripped wires so their ends are even and tighten the new connector.

**TIP: Twist the wires clockwise into a helix, and tighten the nut with a few clockwise turns. To ensure that the splice is secure, gently tug on each wire.**

# 34 · REWIRE A LAMP

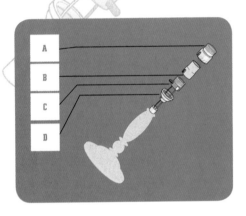

A
B
C
D

When your favorite retro lamp goes on the fritz there's no need to toss it. Rewiring a lamp is an easy job if you use the standardized components found at just about any hardware store.

Start by unplugging the lamp. Then remove the shade and the bulb. Next, disassemble the socket-switch assembly, removing the various parts from the body of the lamp. To do this, separate the following parts from each other: the brass outer shell (A), the insulating sleeve (B), the switch and socket base (C) and the base cap (D). Do this carefully because in many cases the socket is sound and you'll want to reuse it.

Now unscrew the wire terminals and disconnect the cord from the socket. You may have to untie a knot in the cord to remove it from the lamp or, if you're replacing it, cut it and remove the two pieces from either end. Inspect the socket assembly for wear. If it appears sound and you feel the cord was damaged (frayed, mangled, or otherwise compromised), you can reuse the socket assembly. Otherwise replace it with one that matches the type of attachment.

Buy a replacement cord and plug (as a unit) to match the existing length.

You can match the color or select something different—generally you'll find replacement cords in white, black, and transparent. For a two-wire lamp cord, the hot wire has smooth plastic insulation and the neutral wire has ribbed lines in the plastic insulation that run

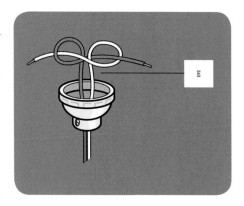

the length of the cord for identification purposes. The identified neutral wire will be connected to the terminal for the wider of the two prongs on a polarized attachment plug.

Reassemble the lamp by running the cut end of the cord up through the lamp. Once it's through, separate the individual wires of the cord at the end, for about 3 inches. Guide these through the body of the socket, strip down the individual wires about $3/4$ inch, then tie an underwriter's knot in the separated wires (see illustration E, above). Twist the stripped ends into tight loops. Wrap clockwise beneath the head of the terminal screws, then tighten the screws to secure the wires. The hot wire connects to the brass-colored terminal and the identified neutral wire connects to the silver-colored terminal. Make sure all the stripped wire is captured under the terminal screw and clip off any extra, including the odd exposed strand.

Secure the shell into the switch body. Finish by sliding any cap assembly over the socket. Now reattach the socket to the lamp body, replace the bulb, plug it in, and let there be light!

# 35 · REPLACE A PLUG

Something as small as an electrical plug can have big consequences. Keep using a damaged plug, and you risk an electrical short or even a fire. But don't toss the appliance; just change the plug.

For a two-wire lamp cord, the hot wire has smooth plastic insulation, and the neutral wire has ribbed lines in the plastic insulation that run the length of the cord for identification purposes. The identified neutral wire will always be connected to the wider of the two prongs on a polarized attachment plug. On two-prong attachment plugs and lamp sockets, the hot wire always connects to the brass-colored terminal and the identified neutral wire always connects to the silver-colored terminal.

The most common type of plug is the simple two-prong, which comes in slip-on or molded varieties. The easiest replacement is a quick-connect plug—you

don't need to separate or strip the wire ends; just slip the cord through the back of the housing with the identified neutral wire aligned with the wide prong on the plug, guide it into the core, and push the prongs closed (1). The core snaps right into the housing and you're good to go. But there's a down side: These are the least durable of replacement plugs.

For a longer-lasting solution, use a standard replacement plug. Remove the damaged plug (cut off a molded plug or disconnect a slide-on type) and separate the cord wires, stripping $^1/_2$ to $^3/_4$ inches of insulation from each wire. Tie the wires in an underwriter's knot (see illustration E, page 71) and connect the ends to the proper terminals on the plug core (2). Finish by screwing the plug core into place.

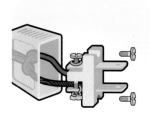

2

The method is roughly the same for replacing a round-cord plug (3), even though they normally include a third, grounding prong. Pop out the disc from the top of the plug and guide the cord through the hole in the plug. Remove about $1^1/_4$ inch of the cord jacket

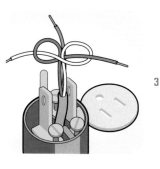

3

and strip the ends of the wires. Now tie an underwriter's knot in the black hot and white neutral wires, and connect the black wire to the brass terminal and the white wire to the silver terminal. Connect the green ground wire to the ground prong and reassemble the plug.

TIP: For safety's sake, always replace a plug with a type that matches the damaged plug.

# 36 · REPAIR A TORN SLIDING SCREEN DOOR

Flies will always find that one hole in any screen, and given the use your screen door sees, sooner or later somebody is sure to punch a hole through it. Keep the flies on the outside where they belong by replacing the screen. (You can use the same process to repair a window screen.)

You'll find all the materials you need for this repair at your local hardware store. Buy enough screen to overlap the doorframe by about 2 inches on each edge. You'll also need new screening spline—the narrow rubber tubing that locks the screen in a groove around the frame. Make sure that the diameter of the new spline exactly matches the existing spline in the door (bring a sample to compare). Lastly, buy a spline-installation tool.

To remove the door, lift it up until the rollers clear the track, then pull the bottom out and lower the door until it clears the top edge of the frame. Find

a flat work surface to lay the door on, then follow this quick and easy process to replace the torn screen:

1. Use an awl to dig out the end of a piece of spline. (It's common to find a separate length of spline on each side of the frame.) Grab this end with your hand and gently pull upward to remove it. Cut the replacement spline to

length with scissors or a utility knife using the pieces you've removed as a guide.

2. Lay the replacement screen over the doorframe. Align one edge of the screen with the outside edge of the door to ensure that the screen is square to the frame.

3. Beginning at one corner, use the convex roller on the tool to press the screen into the groove on a long edge of the doorframe. Use the concave roller on the tool to press the spline into the groove. Apply gentle pressure and angle the tool slightly toward the outside of the frame to avoid tearing the screen. At the opposite edge of the screen, don't form a groove. Instead, gently pull the screen tight as you press the spline in place. Pull straight across the frame to avoid distorting the screen.

After installing all of the spline, use a sharp utility knife to trim the excess screen. Position the knife tip at the junction of the spline and outside edge of the spline groove.

4. Finally replace the door screen in the track. Flies begone!

# 37 · REATTACH A LOOSE DECK PLANK

A loose deck plank is just a stubbed toe waiting to happen. That's why an important part of deck maintenance is resecuring loose planks.

In most cases, the plank just needs to be reattached because the fastener—screw or nail—has worked its way loose within its hole. In some cases, however, the problem is a warped or splitting board—calling for a replacement.

In either case, start by removing the old fasteners. Pry out nails or reverse out screws. Often the screws will be stripped, in which case you should use pliers to turn or pull any free-spinning screws (1).

Replace the fasteners with 3-in. coarse-threaded stainless-steel screws installed through the existing holes (2). If you discover the entire plank needs to be replaced, stain or finish the wood to match, then drill the holes before screwing the new plank into place.

# 38 · PLANT A TREE

. . . . . . . . . . . . . . . . . . . . . . . . . . . . . . . . . . . . . . . . . . . . . . . . . . . . . . . . . . . . . . .

You wouldn't think there would be much to know about planting a tree, right? Dig a hole, drop in the tree, shovel the dirt back in. It turns out there's much more to it—especially if you want the tree to live.

1. The most common mistakes are digging the hole too narrow or too deep. The hole must be two to three times wider than the root ball. And the depth of the hole should equal the distance from the bottom of the root ball up to the root flare, minus 2 inches. (The root flare is where the tree trunk spreads out to form the roots.) Please note that it's crucial not to bury the root flare: doing so can kill the tree or severely stunt the tree's root growth.

2. Roughen the soil at the hole's bottom so that the roots can easily penetrate it. Set the tree into the hole, then remove the twine and burlap from the root ball. Scratch the surface of the root ball with a small cultivator. This will both loosen compacted dirt and expose thousands of tiny roots to the soil.

3. Fertilizers mixed in with the soil can get the tree off to a good start, but too much is worse than none at all. Before adding any, have your soil analyzed and check with the nursery. Then shovel the dirt back in around the root ball, but don't stomp down the soil. Saturate the area with water and add 2 to 4 inches of bark mulch, leaving some mulch-free space around the trunk of the tree. Water regularly for the next 6 to 8 weeks, making sure that the soil is neither dry nor oversaturated.

. . . . . . . . . . . . . . . . . . . . . . . . . . . . . . . . . . . . . . . . . . . . . . . . . . . . . . . . . . . . . . .

# 39 · PRUNE BUSHES AND SMALL TREES

Where your yard is concerned, pruning is the kindest cut. This simple procedure not only gives bushes and trees a pleasing shape and look, it also improves plant health by removing diseased parts and opening the plant to increased light and air circulation.

Before cutting, consult the local agricultural extension office, nursery, or books with your zone information to determine the right time for pruning your particular bush or tree. When you're ready to put your pruners into action, assess the plant for proper proportion and determine where it could benefit from cutting back. Develop a strategy: generally it's best to work from the bottom up, which allows the higher branches you trim away to fall clear rather than getting caught in lower branches. Then, get in close, looking for diseased limbs—obvious candidates for pruning—and for limbs that rub against each other.

Next, choose your tool (when in doubt go for the burlier tool). Small branches can be removed with bypass pruners, which cut without crushing the limb. Midsize branches with diameters starting at about $5/8$ inch are a bit tougher. Use a bypass lopper.

Large branches greater than $7/8$ inch across demand either a pruning saw or a bow saw. The pruning saw's shape and its pull-stroke design make it ideal for getting into tight spots. However, it is limited to branches about 2 inches in diameter. A bow saw cuts on the push stroke, and its larger size allows it to handle bigger branches. Make sure to clean your blades with rub-

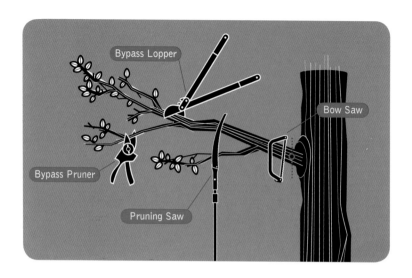

Bypass Lopper

Bow Saw

Bypass Pruner

Pruning Saw

bing alcohol after cutting diseased limbs, or you could spread the malady to your next patient.

When snipping off a small branch on a shrub, cut to just beyond a bud. To reshape or drastically cut back a shrub, use bypass pruners or loppers to prune back to the branch collar, a raised ridge of bark at the base of the branch that contains cells that help close the cut surface. Make a first cut on the bottom of the branch and finish cutting from the top. This prevents a severed branch from tearing off a strip of bark as it falls. Saw to just outside the branch collar. Never leave a stub or stump of a branch.

TIP: Like fine carpentry, successful pruning relies heavily on good equipment. If you want nicely pruned shrubs, invest in good-quality pruning shears and loppers.

Summer can slam that beautiful green carpet outside your front door. These simple steps will see your lawn through even the hottest of times.

1. **Just add water.** A lawn requires at least an inch of water a week—more in windy weather or extreme heat. If you can't water the entire lawn, attend either to areas that boost curb appeal or to those that see the most sun. Two applications per week, $1/2$ inch of water each, are best. Water in the morning. Watering at the peak of the sun uses more water and watering in the evening could contribute to molds.

2. **Hit the deck.** Move your mower's deck up to leave cut grass at least 2 inches high. Taller grass is more stress resistant. The extra height keeps soil cooler and helps shade out weeds.

3. **Sharpen the blade.** A dull blade rips and stresses the grass, leaving the lawn vulnerable to disease and pests. A sharp blade cuts cleanly and helps the lawn resist summer's ravages.

4. **Give it a rest.** When the lawn goes dormant because of extreme heat and dryness, don't cut it. Mowing will just create a lot of dust, not to mention, noise.

# 41 · MIX CONCRETE

Pouring a new sidewalk is much easier than it used to be, thanks to bagged premix concrete. The basic tools of the trade are a wheelbarrow, mortar-mix hoe, 5-gal. plastic bucket, and a mask.

Dump a 60-pound bag of concrete mix into the wheelbarrow followed by a small amount of water. Use the hoe to drag the water-concrete mix to one side of the wheelbarrow, then walk around to the other side and drag it back. Repeat until you have a consistent mixture.

Now comes the tricky part: topping off with just the right amount of water. You want the mixture to be about the consistency of peanut butter. Classic mistake: adding water once the concrete stiffens. This forms watery voids in the mix, which in turn weaken the bonds that form between the calcium silicate hydrates—the glue that binds sand and stone.

You are ready to pour your deck landing or sidewalk, or patch that hole in your garage floor. Cure the poured concrete by keeping it moist for 3 to 7 days—cover it with plastic or sprinkle water on it so the surface stays moist. Unless you want small footprints marring your work, keep the dog and toddlers away.

# 42 · CHANGE A TIRE

Most people think it's the simplest car surgery, but screwing up a tire change can ruin your rig. For starters, park on level ground, kill the ignition, set the brake, and get the spare and tools out of the trunk. "Usually there are ridges in the uni-body where the jack goes," says Ricardo Nault, chief mechanic for Buddy Rice, winner of the 2004 Indy 500. Nault's pit team changes an average of 100 tires a day during practice; they once won the coveted Indy pit-stop competition with a four-tire change time of 4.5 seconds. "Put it in the wrong place and it will damage your frame."

Next, says Nault, break the nuts loose with a wrench, then raise the car and finish unscrewing the nuts by hand. "Now check the spare for debris on the inside and clean it off."

Mount the spare, and tighten the nuts securely with your fingers with just a little nip from the wrench, then lower the car for the final tightening. "Remember to tighten in a star pattern, not a circular one. Imagine a clock, and go from 12 to 7 to 3 to 10 to 5. Otherwise, your wheel can sit off center.

"Finally, the nuts should be tight but not forced. The manufacturers make the wrenches so a small woman can change her tires. The same wrench in a large man's hands could overtorque the nut." And that could lead to deformed tires and dangerous wobbles. So don't go jumping on the wrench.

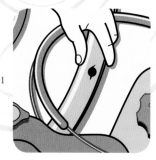

Steam hissing from a ruptured radiator hose? Here's a relatively easy, temporary fix with duct tape.

Open the hood and locate the source of the steam—i.e., the rupture. Wait for the engine to cool off.

1. Clean and dry the area around the fissure; the tape won't stick as well on a damp, dirty surface.

2. Wrap 2 to 3 inches of duct tape around the hose over the hole; press firmly.

3. Overwrap the patch (the hose will be under intense pressure) from 2 to 3 inches above the original piece to about 2 or 3 inches below, then work your way back.

Check your radiator level before cranking the engine. "If it's seriously low and you don't have a can of coolant, use water or, in an emergency, diet soda," says Tony Molla of the National Institute of Automotive Service Excellence and wrench jockey. "Avoid using fruit juice or anything with sugar or acids in it. It'll corrode the radiator and hoses."

# 44 · CHANGE THE OIL AND FILTER

Every 3,000 miles you can commune with your car when you change the oil. First warm the engine to stir up any sediment in the crankcase, then raise the car on stands or ramps. Put a pan under the drain and remove the plug; let it drain for 10 minutes.

Remove the filter, and let it drain into the pan; make sure the O-ring comes off. Use your finger to coat the new filter's O-ring with a little clean oil. If the angle of the new filter allows, prefill it with oil and screw it on. Tighten a three-quarter turn after the gasket touches. Reinstall the drain plug with a new crush washer or seal.

Add all but the last quart of oil, start the engine, and check for leaks. Turn off the car, let it sit for a few minutes, then check the oil level. Top off to the fill mark, and your car is ready to hit the road.

TIP: Most state and local municipalities have regulations about disposal of oil and, in most cases, local service stations must accept oil for recycling. When changing the oil, buy one of the many capture systems available at auto parts stores. These provide a vessel for capturing and transporting the oil.

# 45 · JUMP-START A CAR

This is no idiot's errand, especially with late-model vehicles. Do it wrong and you can fry circuits, short electrical systems, and end up with a sulfuric acid burn. So pay attention! We've corralled Mike Calkins, an ASE certified master technician who oversees all 7,984 AAA-approved repair facilities in North America.

"With any car, make sure the ignition is off and the key is in your pocket. Likewise, if you have aftermarket add-ons like a DVD player, remove those fuses." Consult your owner's manual to see if other fuses need to go.

Make sure the vehicles are parked a couple of feet apart. If they're touching you could create yet another dangerous circuit. "I've seen metal bumpers welded together," Calkins says. Next, turn the live car off and grab your cables—red is for positive, black is for negative.

"First, connect your red cable to the positive terminal of the dead battery, then to the positive side of the live battery. Next connect the negative (black) cable to the negative terminal of the live battery. Warning: Do not connect the cable to the dead car's negative terminal. Instead, connect it to a ground—anything metal that's connected to the engine block will do," says Calkins.

Why so? It can cause sparks and ignite the battery's hydrogen gas. "It happens frequently," Calkins says. "When I was in trade school a student blew the battery top off our instructor's Cadillac."

Start the live car and let it run for a few minutes, giving the dead battery time to charge, and then start the dead car. Remove jumper cables in reverse order, making sure they don't touch each other or a car. Finally, as Calkins points out, with some cars the actual batteries are tucked in strange places—like the trunk—but there should always be a set of terminals under the hood and the same rules apply.

# 46 · SPLICE TWO WIRES TOGETHER

The most secure and durable way to splice two low-voltage wires together is to solder them. Period. Use nothing but 60-40 rosin-core solder intended for electrical wiring. You'll also need some PVC shrink tube. If you're not an old hand at soldering, practice for a dozen or so joints before you tackle the wires you need to splice. Here's a quick how-to:

1. Strip the wires of about $1/2$ inch of insulation. Slip PVC shrink tube over one wire. Twist the two sections of bare wire around each other.

2. Heat the joint with a soldering-iron or -pencil from underneath. Apply solder to the top until molten solder wicks into the joint. Let this cool undisturbed to avoid a "cold" solder joint.

3. Slide the shrink tube over the joint. Use a heat gun to heat the shrink tube to make it shrink down around the wire.

4. Use more shrink tube to bundle multiple connections.

**TIP: Don't have a heat gun and your wife's hair dryer is off-limits? You can make do with a lighter. Be careful not to leave a smudge of conductive carbon over the tubing—and don't use an open flame near any flammable workshop materials or surfaces.**

# 47 · GET A CAR UNSTUCK

When you're stuck, don't gun the engine to get out—the tires will only dig in deeper. Instead, straighten the steering wheel, then dig out as much sand, snow, or mud from around the front or rear of the tires as you can, depending on the direction you want to go. Place a floor mat snugly under a portion of each drive wheel (if your vehicle  is four-wheel-drive, position a mat under each wheel). Ease the vehicle onto the mats. If there's a passenger, have him push the vehicle in the direction you want to go. Repeat the procedure as needed, slowly progressing in the direction of travel until the vehicle is free.

TIP: "To maximize traction, lower the tires' air pressure by 10 to 15 psi or until the sidewall begins to bulge. This spreads out the footprint of the tire, helping the vehicle float over the terrain. Drive slowly and air the tires back up as soon as possible." —Ben Stewart, PM auto editor

# 48 · MASTER PARALLEL PARKING

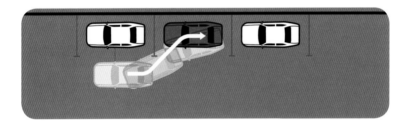

Parallel parking is to driving what chipping is to golf—an inevitable, if often frustrating, part of the game. As the owner/operator of Ann's Driving School in hilly San Francisco, Judy Lundblad makes a living out of destressing the parallel-parking experience. As she puts it, "To parallel park successfully, make sure the space is about 4 to 6 feet longer than your car, then just follow a simple five-step process." (These directions are for a parking space on the right side of the street. Reverse them for a space on the left side.)

1. Signal a right turn. Stop to the side of the car in front of your space so that your side mirror is even with the door of the other car.
2. Look over the shoulder on the side where you are parking, and slowly start turning the wheel to the right as you begin backing in. Aim toward the right rear corner of the space.
3. When your front seat is in line with the rear bumper of the front car, stop and turn the steering wheel one revolution to the left to straighten the tires. Continue backing at this angle until your right front bumper just clears the left rear bumper of the front car.
4. Quickly turn the steering wheel to the left and finish backing into the space.
5. To straighten out, turn the steering wheel one revolution to the right before pulling forward.

The always supportive Lundblad adds, "Getting it right is just a matter of working on your coordination and timing, which is why practice makes perfect when it comes to parallel parking."

# 49 · TIE DOWN A LOAD

"The days of having to mess with a bunch of rope and tying and untying knots are over," says Vaughn Hadenfeldt of Far Out Expeditions (www.faroutexpeditions .com), an adventure travel company based in Bluff, Utah. Hadenfeldt should know. He leads multiday backpacking trips into the wilds of southeastern Utah and provides logistical support for large, months-long archaeological expeditions in this ancient Anasazi country.

Both require truckloads of gear to be hauled securely over bumpy desert roads. Although Hadenfeldt doesn't lead river trips, he uses a lot of river-running gear to tie down loads. "I use cam straps—also called tie-down straps—instead of rope. They are made of nylon webbing with a tightening buckle at the end. Loop them around your roof rack and gear, back through the buckle, and then tighten as hard as you can."

"I also use things called bungee nets that you throw over your gear to keep it secured. Mine are Yakima, because that's who makes my roof racks, but lots of people make them," says Hadenfeldt.

The real key is dryness—and consolidation. "I use large waterproof river bags or huge duffel bags, and I stuff as much as possible in them—sleeping bags, loose gear, whatever—and then I cinch those down. It's better to tie down a few big things than a bunch of little things," says Hadenfeldt. "Whatever you do, don't use tarp," he concludes. "Nothing's worse then seeing some guy driving down the highway with a tarp flapping around on top of his rig—it looks bad and it doesn't keep things dry, either."

TIP: "If the trailer is too low to see, tape sticks or flags to the rear corners." — Mike Allen, PM senior auto editor

# 50 · BACK UP A TRAILER

After parallel parking, backing up a trailer is second on many drivers' lists of most-dreaded activities. Pay attention to these simple tips and proceed with confidence. If you're doing this without a spotter, put your left hand at six o'clock on the steering wheel, and drape your right hand over the seatback. As you back up, move your steering hand in the direction you want the trailer to go.

TIP: Don't leave other drivers guessing. Get a friend to check that the trailer's backup, brake, and turn-signal lights are all in good working order.

# 51 · MANEUVER A CAR OUT OF A SKID

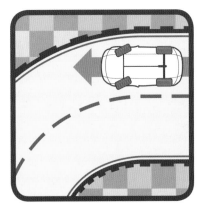

Although there isn't much you can do when your car is pirouetting out of control, you can maneuver out of two basic types of skids before things get messy.

When the front tires slip, you're understeering or plowing (1). This occurs when a motorist takes a turn too fast, at too sharp an angle, or uses the brake or throttle excessively. The tires lose grip and the car's momentum pushes it straight instead of through the curve. When you lose traction up front, steering has no effect; so slow down by gently reducing throttle. The tires will eventually grip and pull you in the direction you want to go.

Rear-wheel slippage is called oversteering or fishtailing (2). It happens during cornering when your rear wheels exceed the limit of their lateral traction before the front tires do, causing the rear of the vehicle to head toward the outside of the corner or front of the car. For rear-wheel slippage, you need to apply "CPR"—correction,

2

pause, and recovery. Correct by steering into the direction of the skid. Pause to let the unsprung weight of the car settle and the tires grip. Recover by steering the car straight; make your movements slow but sure.

**TIP: "Look where you want the car to go. Stare at the pole, and you will hit the pole." —Jeff Robillard, Skip Barber Racing School, Braselton, Ga.**

## 52 · HANDLE A CAR DURING A BLOWOUT

In the category of rude surprises, a high-speed blowout ranks right up there with finding out your girlfriend's a Martian. But, as Eric Espinosa, executive director of the National Institute of Vehicle Dynamics and Drive to Survive, explains, the answer to coming out of this emergency situation unscathed involves doing something that doesn't come naturally.

"Instead of a hitting the brakes, maintain your speed," he says. "Sudden changes of speed can compromise what structural integrity the tire still has—the opposite of what you want to do going 50 or 60 miles an hour."

Of course, it's a matter of finesse. Espinosa stresses, "Press on the accelerator but don't stomp it. You want to keep the car moving so that you can assess the situation for the best opportunity to pull it to the shoulder." He adds, "Do everything smoothly, with as little change to the steering as possible. Any heavy input to the steering is going to deflate the tire."

# 53 · FIX A FLAT ON A BIKE

Glass, nails, thorns—when a sharp object takes the air out of your cycling plans, here's what to do.

Once you remove the wheel, force the deflated tire off the rim, starting opposite the valve, then separate tire and tube. If the leak is a large tear, throw the tube out. To locate a pinhole leak, inflate the tube and feel for escaping air, or

dunk the tube in water and look for bubbles. Apply a patch from the kit you always bring along when biking. The repair should last the life of the tire.

Before remounting the tire, wipe the inside of it clean with a dry cloth to remove any sharp objects that might puncture the tube. Then work the lip of the tire onto half of the rim. Tuck the tube inside the tire, and insert the valve into its rim hole. Pump some air into the tube to reduce its chances of getting pinched between rim and tire. Then work the tire onto the rest of the rim, starting at the valve. Split the wheel into quarters. Work one-quarter down either side from the valve. Repeat the process on the other half of the tire by hand. Although this takes patience, it is preferable to using cheap tire levers, which can abrade or cut the tube.

# 54 · BRAKE A MOTORCYCLE ON A SLICK SURFACE

Physics 101: A two-wheeled vehicle and a slippery blacktop are a bad, bad marriage. But if you absolutely must ride in inclement weather, take every possible precaution.

That starts with your equipment, according to Brooke Lefkow, owner of Naples Motorcycle Riding School in Naples, Florida. "You have to take into account what kind of bike you're riding. For instance, some have antilock braking systems that won't lock up, and a heavier bike is less likely to hydroplane." He adds, "A lot also depends on the condition of the bike; if you have shoddy tires in wet weather, it's going to increase your chances of problems. Your equipment needs to be in good shape."

Lefkow teaches the fundamentals that should be, but often aren't, common sense. "If you're riding at the start of rain, pull over and let it rain for a while, 20 minutes or so. At first, the rain brings up the oil in the road and takes a while to wash it away. The other thing to consider is just pulling over and getting a cup of coffee while you wait for the weather to pass. Or even call it a day."

When it's time to get on your bike, Lefkow advises riding slower, leaving yourself more space than normal for braking, and as always, using both front and back brakes at the same time with steady even pressure. Many riders think the rear brake should be applied first, but the sooner you apply the front brake, the sooner you slow down. Jerking the front brake or hitting the rear break too hard can cause the brakes to lock up and your bike to skid, even in the best road conditions. Don't do it.

# CHAPTER 4

# GLITCH-FREE ELECTRONICS

**T**he 21st century is the age of the digital device. With new innovations being released almost monthly, it's like an extended Christmas for early adopters and tech-lovers of all stripes. Today's devices can help us keep track of our finances and our kids, find and access obscure music and movies, and allow us to participate in global marketplaces without leaving our armchairs.

But as fantastic and high-performance as modern electronics may be, they present challenges on par with their complexity and they are still occasionally subject to the whims of Murphy's law. No device so far is completely immune to a glitch or two, and getting the most out of these miracle machines often entails a quick education. Of course, for anybody who truly loves modern technology, the process of mastering your gear or bringing it back to life is half the fun.

It can also be a matter of necessity. We all have our tech-helpline nightmare stories and, let's face it, customer support is increasingly becoming an afterthought for manufacturers and retailers alike. Best to adopt the old roughneck philosophy: If you need a helping hand, there's one right at the end of your arm.

# 56 · SAFEGUARD YOUR COMPUTER

Viruses and spyware can unleash a host of evils upon your PC, ranging from annoying pop-ups to a zombie system takeover. Security expert John Pironti, President of IP Architects, LLC, suggests a layered approach to protecting your computer.

**Lock it down:** "Go to the security section of your Control Panel and enable the firewall before your PC ever touches the Internet," Pironti advises. Then install a virus protection program and set it to download updates every week.

**Clean it up:** Once a week, do a full virus scan with a program like Symantec's Norton AntiVirus (symantec.com), McAfee VirusScan (mcafee.com), or AVG Anti-Virus (free.grisoft.com). Pironti also says you should run a free spyware checker, such as SpyBot-S&D (safer-networking.org) or Ad-Aware by Lavasoft (lavasoft.com).

# 57 · GET RID OF A VIRUS

Thanks to a bunch of digital vandals and, increasingly, cybercriminals, the Internet is filled with computer-hijacking, mass-mailing worms, viruses, and Trojan Horses. One way to get rid of them is to go to www.symantec.com, click on "Latest Threats," and you'll see a database of computer viruses and excruciatingly detailed descriptions for expunging them.

However, "We *don't* recommend that path," says Kelly Martin, product manager of Symantec's Norton Antivirus software. It turns out that removing a virus might be the easiest way to correct the problem, because all you have to do is simply install the antivirus software—even if a virus has shut down your entire system. "Pop the disk into the CD-ROM slot and then restart the system," says Martin of the company's antivirus product. "It will reboot from the CD, scan for the virus, and remove it."

# 58 · BACK UP ALL YOUR DATA

The moment when that noisy hard drive suddenly goes silent is not the time to be thinking about data back up. Especially since it's so easy to make sure all your important information is copied in a secure place.

**Bombproof backup:** Install an external hard drive the same size as your primary hard drive or larger. When your computer is new, make a drive image with a utility such as R-Drive (drive-image.com), then schedule regular backups using the external drive's software. Multiple computers? Save money with a single network-attached storage (NAS) device, equipped with automatic backup software, which backs up all of the PCs in your network.

If you're a Mac person, you can use the Time Machine feature in the Leopard Operating System to back up your entire hard disk to an external drive. The utility will then automatically back up only what you've changed at regular intervals.

**Online solutions:** If you have a small number of files that don't use up all that much memory, consider online storage services like xdrive.com and mozy.com, which store a copy of all your important data in a remote, secure location.

# 59 · REPLACE YOUR HARD DRIVE

If your hard drive crashes, you might be able to bring it back to life with a reformat. But if it's a physical failure, that sucker's dead and you're going to have to replace it.

No need to book the whole weekend though. According to Branden Keller, owner of www.gameffects.com, a company that builds high-end gaming and design computers, it's easier than changing your car's oil.

Start by unplugging your desktop and removing the screws—usually two—on the back left-hand side. On many desktop machines, it's right below the CD-ROM drive. Wherever it is, it's usually about 8 x 5 x 2 inches and most likely silver or gray. You want to determine if it's an older IDE drive or a modern SATA drive—it's easiest to replace the drive with the same type. A SATA drive uses different cables, and will require a converter cable to work with the IDE's "Molex" power source.

1

1. "In either case, the hard drive will be held in place by a set of screws or by a clip—remove those. You'll see two plugs in the back of it." One is a power plug and one is the data cable. Note the orientation of the pins before unplugging the data cable, and unplug the power cable as well.

2. If you are replacing an IDE drive, things are just a bit more complicated at this point. As Keller says, "Now comes the only tough part. Between the two plugs is another switch with two rows of four pins. The options will be 'Master,' 'Slave,' and 'Cable Select.' Typically, it should be set to 'Master' if you have a single hard drive. If you have two hard drives you'll want to set it to 'Cable Select.' If that doesn't work, you'll have to go back later and select 'Slave.'" SATA drives don't require this setting.

2

3

3. Now, plug those two cables into your new hard drive. "Don't force it. If it isn't going smoothly, you've got it upside down." Put the drive in its slot, replace the panel and screws, and plug in. Fire up the computer and, if the drive was your primary "boot" hard drive, you'll need to boot off your system's installation disk. That is, unless you thought ahead and "imaged" the contents of your original drive onto the replacement—in which case you don't need to reinstall the operating system.

# 61 · EXTEND YOUR WIRELESS NETWORK

You've got a laptop that, ideally, you'd like to use anywhere in your house. But the strength of your wireless Internet fades between floors and behind thick walls. If moving the access point to the center of your home and eliminating all interior walls isn't an option, increase the range of your Wi-Fi by upgrading your equipment. Standard 802.11b and g access points can distribute a computer network to a radius of 130 to 300 feet. But you can squeeze 30 to 80 more feet of range by using an 802.11g access point with MIMO (multiple input, multiple output) technology, or up to 150 extra feet of coverage with an 802.11n access point (a multi-streaming modulation technology that is an improvement over 802.11g access), just make sure that your laptop has an N-capable wireless card installed. You might also consider a dual-band router, which broadcasts with less interference.

If you don't want to replace your equipment, stretch the network through your electrical wiring. Powerline networking hubs (available from Netgear and Linksys) transmit your Internet connection from one outlet to any other in your house. Use them to move your access point to an ideal spot, or to set up a second hotspot for more coverage.

# 62 · REMOVE A STUCK CD

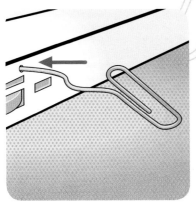

There's something uniquely frustrating about a CD or DVD stuck in a drive. Fix the problem by starting with the easiest possible solution, then trying increasingly more complex approaches.

First, check that the power is on, then make sure the disk is in the drive. With the "duh" factor accounted for, try a software solution. According to Joey Jasion, special weapons agent 443 for the Geek Squad, "On a Windows machine, double-click on 'My Computer' and navigate to the CD-ROM icon, right-click and select 'Eject.' If you have a Mac, reboot while holding down your mouse button."

Next try a manual solution. Jasion suggests: "The most common way to get the CD out is to stick a paper clip in the little hole next to the tray door; it's a manual release mechanism. Even if you have a slot drive, look right inside the felt barrier or door hatch—there's probably a hole on one side or the other."

Jasion adds, "In the worst-case situation, you'll need to open up the computer and disassemble the CD or DVD drive." Which, depending on your technical ability, may be a job for somebody like Agent Jasion.

# 63 · ENCRYPT AN E-MAIL

According to Lawrence Rogers, senior member of the technical staff at Carnegie Mellon Software Engineering Institute's CERT Program, the key lies in, well, keys. "Download publicly available software called PGP; it works with most PC systems on Outlook or Thunderbird (the software is also available for Macs)," Rogers says. "Then you'll need to create two keys—one public and one private."

You upload the public key to a public key server—the PGP program will be able to find these servers. Then, according to Rogers, "You create a private key that you protect with a 'pass phrase,' basically a password on steroids. This key you give to no one."

Here's where you get to channel James Bond. To send someone an encrypted e-mail, you use the public key they've created and uploaded, which matches their private key. The public key encrypts the e-mail (or a file you attach to the e-mail) and the recipient uses their private key to decode the message when they get it. Use the process in reverse to receive an encrypted e-mail or attachment. If you prefer web-based e-mail programs, consider Hushmail (hushmail.com), a free service that encrypts all of its users' e-mails.

# 64 · INSTALL A GRAPHICS CARD

If you want to play with the big boys
and the latest hi-res software, your
computer is going to need a little
help in the video-processing department. Here's how to give it a leg up.

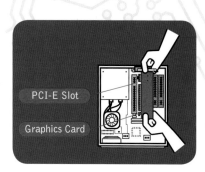

PCI-E Slot

Graphics Card

1. Check inside your PC. To
   determine what card fits in your
   computer, open it up and take
   a look at the motherboard. Your PC should have a dedicated graphics slot
   that fits either a PCI-E (Peripheral Component Interconnect Express) or
   AGP (Accelerated Graphics Port) card. PCI-E is the more advanced of
   the two technologies.

2. Consider your monitor. Different graphics cards have different combina-
   tions of outputs. Most common are VGA, DVI, DisplayPort, HDMI, and
   a multipurpose video expansion port. Make sure to purchase one that
   matches your monitor.

3. Pick a card. Graphics cards range in price from $50 to more than $650,
   and performance and accessories vary accordingly. If you'd like a no-
   ticeable bump up in video processing, we'd suggest at least 256MB.

4. Insert card into the slot. Push firmly until it clicks into place. Plug your
   monitor into the back of the card—not your old monitor port. Turn your
   PC on and install your card's drivers. Adjust the screen to your preferred
   resolution in the control panel.

# 65 · TAKE THE PERFECT PORTRAIT WITH A DIGITAL POINT-AND-SHOOT

While your portraits (and probably your subjects) are unlikely to achieve Annie Leibovitz–worthy glam, you can learn to take a decent portrait. Artistic genius is not required—the key lies in a mastery of focal lengths and remembering to turn on the flash.

"You want to use a longer focal length (more zoom) than normal— and normal is roughly what your naked eye sees. On a camera, normal is about 50mm," says Lynn Donaldson, a professional photographer who shoots for the *New York Times, People,* and *National Geographic Traveler.* "If you go wider than 50mm you will exaggerate features—like making someone's nose look disproportionately bigger. *Not* flattering." On the other hand, if you zoom in too much you can add weight because longer lenses compress space.

"A pretty safe, flattering focal length for portraits is 120 to 150mm. " The problem, though, is that many digital cameras don't always tell you what your lens is magnified to. For that, consult your owner's manual for focal lengths. "Most point-and-shoots don't go over 150mm, so in that case push the zoom out as far as it will go.

"Make sure your background is simple, and avoid shooting in bright light, because people squint, and you get the worst expressions that way. Also, don't stand with the subject's back to the sun. With automatic cameras, the background will be properly exposed but your subject's face will be underexposed and come out dark.

"To counteract this, turn the flash *on*. This adds 'fill flash' (unless your camera has a 'fill flash' mode, in which case use that) and it's essential when shooting someone in a cowboy or baseball hat in the sun. Otherwise, they end up with a black mask looking like Zorro. Actually, you can almost always use your flash in the sun—it evens out skin tones, and makes wrinkles and dark circles disappear. It's flattering. The trick to not making your image too bright is to stand back and zoom in—at 120 to 150mm you should be safe." You can also opt to use the continuous exposure or "burst" mode if your camera has one. Then just pick out the shot you like best.

# 66 · RETOUCH DIGITAL PHOTOS

Some shots are too flawed to fix with a click on "autocorrect." Here's how to perform simple surgery on digital images with nearly any photo-editing software, such as Picasa or Paint.Net for Windows machines, and iPhoto for the Mac.

**Cropping:** Even a small spot of deep black or bright color can throw off a program's ability to balance an image's light or color levels. Crop out unwanted elements before making image-wide adjustments.

**Color temperature:** If the color adjustment can't fix unnatural colors, such as a sickly green from fluorescent lights, and there's no time to tweak the red, green, and blue levels, there's a last resort—declare yourself an artist and switch the image's mode to black-and-white.

**Lighting:** Too much flash? Reduce the brightness and increase the contrast. For poorly lit images, do the opposite, boosting the brightness and reducing the contrast. To avoid gray, hazy images, make sure the photo's black elements are still black and the whites still white.

**Red-eye:** If your software doesn't have a red-eye reduction feature, zoom in on the offending eyes until you can see individual pixels. Select the desaturation tool and dab at the red portion of each eye. This drains the color, turning reds into grays, while retaining highlights so the irises don't look artificial. The results probably won't be pretty, but boring gray beats demonic red.

# 67 · INSTALL A SECURITY CAMERA

If you want to keep watch over your domain and all that goes with it, you should put in your own security surveillance. The first decision is whether to go with a hardwired system, or wireless. Wireless systems are simpler to use and less expensive. You simply mount the cameras, follow the instructions for setting up the software, and

you're good to go. Companies such as D-Link (dlink.com) and Logitech (www.wilife.com) provide complete packages with cameras and software. The camera sends the signal to your computer and you can check exterior views any time you want. Many people, however, still choose a hardwired system to avoid interference with the video signal and because they believe it is more secure. In either case you need to start by choosing where to position your cameras.

Camera location depends on what you're trying to detect. If you're worried about burglars, you might want to cover the perimeter of the house. If your driveway trophy '69 Mustang is the concern, a garage cam is the answer.

Regardless of where you locate the camera, keep it out of reach. Jeff Shotlander, North American account manager for Swann Communications, explains why. "You want to mount the cameras high enough so that they can't be messed with, but where you still have maximum visibility." Shotlander also suggests purchasing a camera that can see where and when you want it to, even in the dark. "All cameras on the market today are pretty much color. If you want to see in the dark, you need to get a camera with infrared, or IR illuminators. These are basically LEDs that surround the lens and allow the camera to see in the dark. The rule of thumb is one foot of nighttime viewing for every LED. The image is black-and-white at night with the IR illuminators."

Most hardwired systems are sold as turnkey packages, so mounting hardware and cables are included. To install, mount the camera with the supplied brackets and drill a hole through the wall where you want the cable to enter your home.

The cable itself is what's known as a "Siamese," meaning it carries a low-voltage power line for the camera running alongside a line for video feed. Cables and extensions are offered in preset lengths, so you can run it to wherever you need it. As Shotlander says, "It's all plug and play." The final choice is where you plug and play. Shotlander chose a passive setup for his own home. "I connected my cameras to a digital video recorder (DVR) because I travel—I more or less catch the event after it happens. My DVR runs all the time; it records to the hard drive as opposed to a tape, so the quality is much better.

Both hardwired and wireless systems can be used over the Internet, increasing the flexibility and surveillance potential of any system you chose. There are other options: If you don't want the camera on full-time, you can set it to react to motion. You could also connect a DVR to a TV input jack, so you can slyly switch over to view whoever is ringing your doorbell.

# 68 · SPLICE IN CABLE CONNECTIONS

The cable company ain't the boss of you. Don't pay the price for a technician to cut and run a line to your TV's new location—do it yourself.

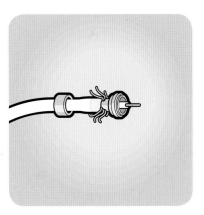

All you'll need is good-quality coaxial-cable strippers and a crimper (if you're using crimped connectors rather than the screw-on types). First, cleanly cut the cable where you want to add a connection. Now strip down the insulation around the center wire about $1/2$ inch, and cut about $1/8$ inch of the outside insulation, exposing the wire braid and metal sheath underneath. Slide the crimped or F connector onto the end of the cable (often this is two pieces, a shell that is crimped, and the actual connector body that slides into the shell before it is crimped), and use the crimper to crimp the connector securely onto the cable.

You can also use screw-on connectors, though they tend to be a little less reliable. Strip the outside insulation down about $1/2$ inch, then bend the wire and metal insulation down over the outside of the cable and cut the foam insulation away from the central wire. Now just screw the connector down tightly and your splicing is complete—you are cable ready.

*Upscaling DVD players can effectively increase the resolution of a standard DVD. It's a trick, but often a very good one.

**When an HD antenna is attached directly to an HDTV, a coaxial cable transmits a hi-def signal, at up to 1080p.

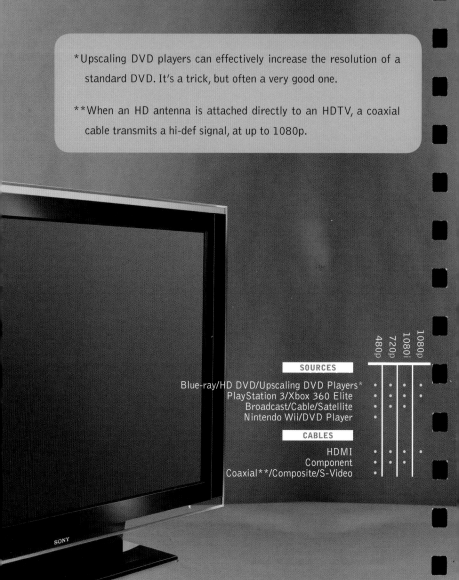

| | 480p | 720p | 1080i | 1080p |
|---|---|---|---|---|
| **SOURCES** | | | | |
| Blue-ray/HD DVD/Upscaling DVD Players* | • | • | • | • |
| PlayStation 3/Xbox 360 Elite | • | • | • | |
| Broadcast/Cable/Satellite | • | • | • | |
| Nintendo Wii/DVD Player | • | | | |
| **CABLES** | | | | |
| HDMI | • | • | • | • |
| Component | • | • | • | |
| Coaxial**/Composite/S-Video | • | | | |

SONY

# 69 · HOOK UP AN HDTV

Hi-def televisions have the potential to produce some staggeringly bad images if hooked up incorrectly. In the era of digital television, resolution is quantifiable, but high-res has to be coaxed into its glory through a combination of the proper cables, components, and source material. The top prize: a breathtakingly crisp 1080p (1920 x 1080 progressively scanned pixels) widescreen picture. You can't always get picture perfection, but by following this chart you can hook up components the right way—ensuring that your set is squeezing the most resolution possible out of any video source.

Note the TV's maximum resolution, then check the chart for the maximum resolution of each source. When connecting these components to the TV, use the cable that matches the resolution you're dealing with. If your TV's resolution is less than the source's, or you're using a cable that downgrades the signal, you won't get the best picture. For example, if you have a 1080p TV and a Blu-ray player (also 1080p), but you use a composite cable to connect them, you won't get the best signal. HDMI is almost always the best choice, because the signal is uncompressed 1080p. Finally, don't buy pricey HDMI cables. The price increases for extra-long cables, but otherwise, go for the cheapest ones. Your TV won't know the difference . . . because there isn't any.

# 70 · HANG A FLAT-PANEL TV

The only thing cooler than a flat-panel TV is a flat-panel TV that appears to be floating on the wall. And the slickest way to do that is to run the cables inside the wall. Here's a description of how it's done.

1. Establish a safe work area by removing furniture and other valuable items, such as children and pets, that may be damaged or create tripping hazards during your installation. Measure and mark off the area where you'll be mounting the TV. Use a stud finder to locate studs, and mark with a pencil. (Check the specifications for your TV to determine how many studs you'll need; some TVs require more studs for support due to their weight.)

2. Drill a couple small "pre-holes" to ensure you're hitting the stud, then hold the mount up and drill in four 3-in. lag screws to secure the mount to the stud. Check the mount with a level before proceeding.

3. Cut a small (4 in. x 2 in.) hole below the mount using a drywall knife or saw. Now stick a Glo-Rod into the hole and check if there are any fire blocks running down the wall between the studs.

4. If you encounter a fire block (a horizontal member positioned between two studs), use a flex bit on your drill to bore a hole through the fire block, being careful that the bit doesn't skid off the fire block and make a hole in the wall. Now check with the Glo-Rod to see that you have un-impeded access down into the wall cavity, and cut another access hole about 1 foot up from the floor.

5. Use the Glo-Rod to pull the TV cables up through the wall. (Standard power cords cannot be run inside the wall because of building and safety codes. So even after you've managed to run the cable and mount the TV, you'll still need to have a licensed electrician install an outlet behind the TV to supply the power.)

6. Finish the job by installing appropriate wall plates for the cables, top and bottom. Now you just connect and mount the TV and you're good to go.

Ah, but there is an easier way. If you fear your floating flat-screen fantasy might come crashing down on you, use the procedure described above for installing the TV mount (steps 1 and 2). But rather than hiding the cables in your wall, run the cables inside a cable conduit attached to the wall instead. Cable conduits come in flexible and rigid styles, in a variety of colors—and some are even paintable.

**TIP: Save your back and buddy up. OSHA recommends that anytime you hang a TV over 32 inches, you should use two people for the job.**

# 71 · SET UP A HOME THEATER

"I got tired of having friends over for movies and having only two seats in the 'sweet spot,'" says Keith Kirkpatrick, a conference director from New York City. So Kirkpatrick converted his small apartment's living space into a home theater with stadium seating. It's an inspiration for men everywhere yearning for their own cine-shack.

To get the seating levels just right, Kirkpatrick geeked out and bought the obscure book *Stadia: A Design and Development Guide.* On eBay, he swiped six cushy movie-theater seats for $20 each. Luckily, you can skip the book and use Kirkpatrick's seating placements as a guide.

Keith's first row is his couch—Hef style—followed by two rows of three seats. He built two seating platforms out of basic 3 x 6 ft. MDF board ($3/4$ in. thick) and raised them 18 inches and $26^1/2$ inches off the ground, respectively, using customized table legs from www.tablelegsonline.com (seriously).

"That's based on an average height of 5'10", plus a few extra inches. I've got a lot of tall friends so I wanted to be able to see over them."

Enter the components. "Your receiver is the brains of your system. Everything runs off that—DVD player, speakers—so make sure you read your owner's manuals about connecting components." Kirkpatrick's ethic is good quality while not breaking the bank. He used an old receiver, but for hi-def you'll want a receiver with plenty of HDMI inputs. He bought a $900 InFocus projector—but you can go really wild with this purchase if you choose; high-end models can cost as much as $25,000. Although Kirkpatrick settled on an $8.99 projection screen from Kmart, here again, you can spend thousands on top-of-the-line projection screens.

Kirkpatrick went with the classic 5.1 formula for speaker placement: one in each front corner, plus a center channel in front, and another pair in the rear. (If you want to go all out, use a more up-to-date 7.1 system.) To calibrate his speakers and nail the sweet spot, he used a Home Theater Calibration Disc by Discwasher.

So, now that it's hooked up, what's Kirkpatrick's favorite surround-sound experience? "The opening scene of *Saving Private Ryan,* with the bullets whizzing right by your head is pretty intense."

# CHAPTER 5

# KING OF THE CASTLE

If you want to just eat, takeout may be the way to go. But if you want to eat well, you have to learn your way around the old cooktop. And, as with other home improvement projects, ruling in the kitchen requires knowledge of both the tools and the techniques they were built for.

You'll see, operating in the culinary zone is not the drudgery you might think; it's actually a chance to exercise your creativity and impress family, friends, and your significant other along the way. Whether you're making an omelet or getting your beef fix with the perfect steak, cooking is all about satisfying your taste buds as well as your hunger. So get ready to exercise your prowess with things sharp and hot, and bring your hunger—this is the only section in the book where the mistakes are edible.

Of course, being a well-rounded man also means knowing how to take care of pesky home-ec challenges like sewing on a button and cleaning the taco sauce off your favorite shirt. Happily, opening a bottle of the bubbly is part of the essential skill set, too.

# 72 · CLEAN A CAST-IRON PAN

"A cast-iron skillet is like the utility infielder of cookware," says Mark Kelly, marketing promotions manager for Lodge Manufacturing, the sole U.S. manufacturer of cast-iron cookware. "But unlike a utility infielder, the cast-iron skillet plays every day."

That's because cast iron has superior heat-retention properties. But cast-iron cookware needs to be properly maintained, and that means cleaning it without removing the "seasoning."

Most manufacturers season cast-iron cookware at the point of origin, a process whereby the surface is coated with cooking oil and then heated so that the oil seals the microscopic pits and pores of the metal. Still, it doesn't hurt to season the skillet before you first use it, by coating it with a little vegetable oil and warming over a low flame or in an oven on low heat.

Then, when washing, easy does it. As Kelly puts it, "Just use warm water and a nylon scrub brush. Hardened materials are removed with either a wooden scrubber or a nylon scrubber." He adds, "The more you cook with it the more the surface becomes nonstick and the easier it will be to clean. Some people use a very mild soap but we recommend just using warm water and a nylon scrub brush because soap can clean off the seasoning. And you should never put a cast-iron piece in the dishwasher." If that leaves you worrying about bacteria, don't. As Kelly points out, "The cookware gets to over 500 degrees F, so any bacteria is going to be eliminated."

# 73 · SCOUR A MICROWAVE OVEN

Have you been avoiding this job so long that the inside of your microwave looks like the back end of a junior high school food fight? Procrastinate no longer; let the microwave do most of the work!

Fill a microwave-safe bowl with water and $1/4$ cup lemon juice or vinegar (whichever smell says "clean" to you), then microwave on high until the mixture boils, 2 to 5 minutes. Let sit for a minute or two to allow the steam to do its thing, then remove the bowl and clean the interior with a dishtowel or other rough-textured cloth. Even baked-on food mess should be easy to remove after the steam bath. If any tough spots remain, tackle those with a damp sponge and a little dish soap—save abrasive or chemical cleaners for the bathroom.

Remove the carousel tray and wash it in the sink in warm soapy water. And be sure to remove any dust or kitchen build-up from the rear vents of the microwave.

You're on your way out the door when you suddenly discover that the only thing between you and respectability is that ugly stain dead center on your shirt. Time to act.

Different stains require different solutions, but some general rules apply to all of them. Treat the stain as quickly as possible, blotting if the stain is still wet, but never rubbing— that will just make a bad situation worse. It's always a good idea, whether you're working with upholstery fabric or clothing, to test any solution on an out-of-the-way area. Treatments for some common stains include:

**Blood:** Move fast and use cold water. Rinse with a mild detergent and, if that doesn't completely do the trick, give the stain a shot of Windex (for its ammonia) and soak it in cold water. Last resort: hydrogen peroxide before a final cold water soak. Then wash normally in cold water; don't heat-dry unless the stain is gone.

**Wine:** Blot the wine as soon as it spills, then dab the stain with a clean cloth moistened in a half-and-half solution of dishwashing liquid and hydrogen peroxide. Be conservative at first and repeat if necessary. Air-dry the fabric and repeat the process if the stain is still visible.

**Coffee:** Soak thoroughly as soon as you detect the stain and then scrub with a mild detergent. (Many cleaning experts swear by Dove soap for its lack of additives; use a bar as scrubber and soap all in one.) A coffee stain can usually be cleaned out, even if it takes a couple washings.

**Fruit:** Stretch the stained material over a cup and pour boiling water through the stain. If you've acted quickly while the stain is still wet, this should take care of it. If not, blot the stain with a sponge soaked in lemon juice cut with water.

**Grease:** A little baking soda on top of the grease stain will soak out some of the offending substance, but then it's time to go deep. Coat the stain with dishwashing soap ("cuts grease" is the number one claim, right?), now blot the stain with a clean cloth soaked in cold water, drying the surface with a dry cloth or towel. The dry towel is to suck up the dissolved grease. You may have to repeat this several times, but don't be tempted to soak the whole shirt in water and dish soap—the grease may dissolve and travel. Finally, wash the shirt after pretreating the spot with dish soap for 5 to 10 minutes.

**TIP: Upholstery can be tricky to spot clean—the fabric itself may contain treatments that determine how it should be cleaned. When in doubt, check the tag. Most upholstered pieces come with a code printed on the furniture tag: *W* means safe to clean with water, *S* means dry-clean only, and *X* means vacuum only.**

# 75 · SEW ON A BUTTON

As any man knows, dress-shirt buttons are pre-programmed to pop off on the morning of the big meeting. It's one of those laws Murphy laid down. Don't be caught short: keep a portable sewing kit handy. With a little patience and a steady hand, you'll be looking sharp in no time.

First you'll need to choose a spool of thread that matches the color of your shirt and thread 18 inches of it through the eye of a needle, forming two strands of equal length. Roll the ends together to make a knot, then rub the thread with candle wax. "It won't tangle as much," explains wardrobe designer Marc Borders.

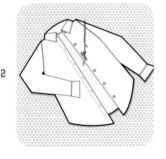

1. To sew on the button, begin by pushing the needle up through the fabric where the button will be, extending the thread fully to anchor the knot.

2. Slide the button over the needle and down the thread onto the fabric. Place a safety pin between the button and fabric as a temporary spacer.

3. Thread the needle back down through another hole in the button and through the fabric. If the button has four holes, you can create a cross with your thread or a parallel pattern—see how the other buttons on the garment are secured and note the style. For the cross pattern, pass the needle and thread up through one hole and down through the diagonal hole, then up through the adjacent hole and down through the hole diagonal to it. To create a parallel pattern, pass the needle and thread up though one hole and down through the next hole, then, moving clockwise, go up through the next hole and down through the last hole.

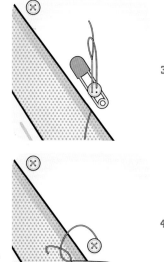

3

4

4. Repeat until you're almost out of thread, then bring the needle up through the cloth, remove the safety pin, and wrap the thread six times around the other strands underneath the button. Thread the needle back down through the cloth, cut the needle free, and get to that meeting.

TIP: If you have to replace a button on a heavy-use garment like an overcoat, go with a heavier gauge thread, such as quilting thread. You can buy waxed quilting thread to make the job even easier.

# 76 · CHANGE A DIAPER

If you're okay with cleaning gunk out of gutters, diapers should be no problem. Lay the baby on his or her back on a firm, padded surface with side railings (or on the floor or bed). Always keep at least one hand on the child at any time to prevent him from surprising you with his rolling abilities. Unfasten the diaper. With one hand gently grasp the baby by the ankles, raise the baby's bottom, and slide out the used diaper. Still holding the ankles, clean the baby's bottom with a sanitary wipe or a warm, wet cloth, wiping downward to keep the genitals clean. Slide the new diaper under the baby, lower the legs and release the ankes; fold up and fasten the diaper. Wrap up the used diaper and dispose of it as soon as humanly possible. Whew!

**TIP: If you have a son, do yourself a favor and keep his manhood covered during the diapering process—you don't want to be caught in a surprise shower!**

# 77 · FIRE UP A CHARCOAL GRILL

A backyard cookout is an essential rite of summer, but it can be an exercise in frustration if you can't get your charcoal mojo working. Meat expert Bruce Aidells relies on the time-tested physics of the chimney starter, a punctured-steel cone with a handle. Fill the top with charcoal, the bottom with wadded-up newspaper, light it, and in no time you'll have red hot coals. But Aidells, host of the cooking show *A View from the Bay,* co-author of *The Complete Meat Cookbook,* and author of *Bruce Aidells's Complete Sausage Book,* emphasizes that starting the coals is just one step. Setting up your grill is equally important.

A chimney usually doesn't hold enough coals for grilling a full grill's worth of meat, so Aidells creates a base of coals over which he dumps the starter coals when they are ready. "Control heat intensity by how deep the coals are," he says. "Look at the basic kettle grill as a circle: maybe a half of the circle will have coals piled three to four layers thick, and perhaps a quarter will have a couple layers thick, then another portion of the grill will have no coals at all. Measure the heat with your hand about 2 to 3 inches above the grill; if you can leave it there for no longer than a count of two, that's a good grilling temperature. Where there are fewer layers of coals, the grill is cooler. The idea is if you're cooking something like a steak and it's cooking too quickly you move it to a cooler area of the grill." This method requires some trial and error, but experiment with your setup and you'll be the neighborhood grill master in no time.

# 79 · OPEN THE BUBBLY

If your idea of opening a bottle of champagne (or sparkling wine) entails letting the cork fly and sloshing as much foamy overflow into nearby glasses as quickly as possible, well, you need to think again. Champagne may be a lot more fun than Chianti, but opening the bottle still requires a measure of subtlety and elegance.

David Munksgard, winemaker for California's Iron Horse Vineyards, knows only too well how precious those bubbles are. "We work really hard at getting bubbles in there, and the bubbles that are held within the wine itself are held quite lightly. Sudden opening allows surface pressure to escape too rapidly. That's why champagne should be opened with a whisper rather than a bang."

1. Start by removing the foil hood that covers the wire cage, which in turn covers the cork. Many people untwist and remove the cage, but not Munksgard. "I was trained to just remove the foil so it looks nice," he says.

2. and 3. "Then untwist the wire cage and use it as a handle to hold onto the cork as you turn the bottle on a 45-degree angle," the winemaker instructs. He cautions to

turn the bottle in only one direction to lessen the possibility of tearing the cork and sending pieces of cork into the wine. You can use a towel or napkin to help you keep your grip on the bottle and cork and to contain any overflow.

4. "Start to release the cork while applying firm and steady back pressure. It's a very controlled process at that stage, because after you break that little bit of a seal from that cork being in there awhile, it will naturally be forced out of the bottle. Slowly remove the cork and keep control of it, and pour without wasting a drop!"

**TIP: When it comes to the bubbly, always stay chill. Munksgard recommends, "Before serving, chill the wine for several hours in a fridge at 40 to 45 degrees F, or for half an hour in a bucket of ice and water. Chilled bubbly tastes better, looks better, and those precious bubbles last longer when chilled."**

# 80 · CARVE A TURKEY

If you're like most of us, you only face carving the bird once a year—which is why most of us can do little more than hack off misshapen hunks of meat in wildly varying thicknesses. But follow these four simple steps and you, too, can create the Norman Rockwell platter of artistically arranged, dime-thin turkey slices to present to your family.

Mary Clingman, director of the Butterball Turkey Talk-Line tells how. "It starts with the knife, and the knife has to be sharp. You can use an electric knife, but I personally prefer a regular knife because it's not quite as big and I feel like I have more control over what I'm doing. An 8- or 10-inch carving knife is great." And be sure that you don't overcook the bird because dried out turkey meat is bound to shred, rather than slice neatly. (See Skill #84: Roast a Turkey, page 152.)

After cooking, let the turkey "rest" for 10 to 15 minutes before you start slicing it. This time allows the tasty juices to be redistributed throughout the bird. From there, Clingman offers these instructions:

1. First, remove the legs. Grab hold of a drumstick with one hand and place a knife between the thigh and body. Cut through the skin and straight down, all the way to the thigh joint, and the leg will come right off. Repeat. Now separate the thigh and drumstick at the joint and place them on a serving platter.

2. Insert a fork in the upper wing to steady the turkey. Make a long horizontal cut above the wing joint through to the body. If you want, you can remove the wings entirely and add them to the serving platter; first cut off and discard the tips.

3. Now for the white meat. Beginning halfway up the breast, slice straight down with an even stroke. When the knife reaches the wing joint, the first slice of meat will fall free.

4. Continue to slice the breast meat, starting the cut at a higher point each time. The thickness of the slices is a matter of personal preference, but once you choose a gauge, do your best to stick with it. Arrange the slices of white meat neatly on your platter with the rest of the skillfully carved turkey. Time for that Norman Rockwell moment.

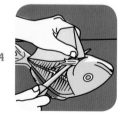

Set the scene with a flat surface and an appropriate knife—any long, thin, flexible, and sharp blade will do, but for larger fish you might need a stiffer blade. Make your first cut behind the pectoral fin or gill cover, angling the tip of the knife slightly toward the head.

1. Cut down to the spine, but not through it.

2. Next, turn the fish end to end and run your knife head to tail along the dorsal fin and backbone, pushing the knife deep enough to bounce the blade off the fish's rib cage.

3. Then run the knife carefully over the rib cage until you reach the spine. Pull the fillet back as you cut, which will help you see what you're doing.

4. Repeat the process through the bottom half of the fish, and you're done with that side. Flip and repeat for two boneless fish fillets.

**TIP: "One side of the fish is always easier to cut than the other. It's a matter of physiology: Right-handed people find it easier to cut from left to right; lefties, vice versa. Do the harder side first." —John Steadman, owner and operator of Point to Point Outfitters, a charter boat service on Long Island, NY.**

# 82 · MAKE THE PERFECT OMELET

· · · · · · · · · · · · · · · · · · · · · · · · · · · · · · · · · · · · · · · · · · · · · · · · · · · · · ·

If eggs are nature's perfect food, then an omelet is the egg in perfect form. Want to satisfy a craving for one without a trip to the diner? Then you'll need to follow the sage advice of Howard Helmer, a man who's spent 40 years touting the benefits of the egg for the American Egg Board. (He also happens to hold the Guinness Book record for the world's fastest omelets.)

For Howard, it starts with the pan. "Most chefs use an 8-inch omelet pan, but I prefer a 10-inch pan," he says. "Any decent pan will do as long as it has some kind of quick-release finish, such as Teflon or similar coating."

Howard's recipe for the "egg batter" is the height of simplicity: 2 eggs mixed with 2 tablespoons of water. "I use water rather than milk because it makes for a lighter omelet and the batter moves around in the pan more easily," he explains. "Remember, in an omelet the egg is just a package for the filling."

**TIP: When making multiple omelets for a brunch, use Howard's trick for achieving perfect portions. "Make the batter using 2 eggs and 2 tablespoons of water for each person. When pouring the omelet into the pan, use a standard 4-ounce soup ladle, which will hold exactly one omelet's worth of eggs."**

To create the perfect omelet, Howard offers these steps:

1. Heat the pan on high heat. (Howard says, "I hold my hand near the lip of the pan. If I can feel the heat coming off it, it's ready.")

2. Drop a pad of butter or margarine into the pan and coat the bottom with it. Don't use oil—it gives the omelet a slippery feel in the mouth.

3. Pour in the egg batter. If the pan is hot enough, the edges should set immediately.

4. Use an inverted spatula to draw the edges in toward the center and, at the same time, tilt the pan so that the uncooked egg runs over the hot pan surface just exposed (a process Helmer calls "Digging a hole and filling it up"). Do this all the way around until there is no uncooked egg left, but the top is still wet.

5. Add whatever ingredients you want along one half of the omelet (left-hand side for right-handers, and vice versa). Then use the spatula to fold the other side over the ingredients. Finally, turn the whole pan upside down onto the plate. Serve the omelet immediately.

# 83 · GRILL A FLAWLESS STEAK

It's the carnivore's dream meal: the perfectly grilled steak. Reaching this culinary pinnacle means starting with a great piece of beef. And when the best steaks are the question, it's only natural to turn to the king of all things grilled, Steven Raichlen, author of *The Barbecue Bible* and *How to Grill,* and the host of the PBS series *Primal Grill with Steven Raichlen.* His advice? "The best meat is prime grade, dry-aged for a richer flavor, and a cut that is intrinsically tender, such as New York strip or rib eye."

Next comes the seasoning, and as far as Raichlen is concerned, the simpler the better: "Coarse sea salt and freshly ground pepper applied right before it goes on the grill." As for the grill, he recommends preheating to high, "Unless it's a really thick steak, like a 2-in.-thick porterhouse. In that case you want half of the grill on high and half on medium. Sear it on each side over high heat, and then move it to the medium heat to cook it through."

Beyond that, it's all about using heat skillfully to get the steak to your preferred state of doneness. Raichlen says, "I use the 'rule of palm': anything thicker than the palm of your hand viewed sideways should be cooked with the grill lid closed. Otherwise, keep the grill lid open." He adds, "To determine how done the steak is, use the poke test—poke the surface of the steak: soft and squishy is rare, somewhat yielding is medium rare, pretty firm with just a little bit of yield is medium, and hard and springy is well done."

And to finish, Raichlen recommends, "Let the steak sit for a few minutes before serving, and burnish it with a little oil or butter to bring out the flavor." Bon appétit!

**TIP: More rules from Raichlen: "Turn don't stab! Use tongs—not a fork—for turning the steak. Poking holes in a steak lets those tasty juices escape."**

# 84 · ROAST A TURKEY

Cooking the Thanksgiving Day turkey is one of those challenges that separates the clued-in from the clueless. Start with the right bird for your crowd. Rick Rodgers, cooking writer and teacher, and author of *Thanksgiving 101,* suggests, "Allow about one pound per person. That way, you're sure to have enough for leftovers or seconds." But there's more to buying your bird than just the poundage.

"If you can, look inside the wrapper to see what you're getting," Rodgers says. "You don't want a bird with a tear or imperfection in the skin. I also buy fresh rather than frozen because I like that clean natural taste."

Once you've brought your flawless bird home, don't skimp on the equipment. Rodgers uses a good-quality pan with a V-shaped roasting rack and you should, too. Cheap aluminum throwaways are for tailgate party lasagna, not a holiday centerpiece.

The turkey should sit above the juices so it doesn't stew and fall apart. Rodgers also stresses the need for a good meat thermometer. "The pop-up thermometer can get glued shut with the basting juices. You can buy a reliable instant-read thermometer from the supermarket for about six bucks." He also has some inside advice for anyone looking to avoid the shame of a dried-out turkey. "Dark meat is fatty and the leaner breast meat gets done before the dark meat, so I cover the breast area with a piece of aluminum foil, leaving the wings and thighs exposed. The heat bounces off the foil, and the foil will capture a little steam underneath to keep the turkey moist."

The turkey should be sitting breast-up on the rack when you slide it into an oven preheated to 325 degrees F. Rodgers advises cooking the turkey 20 minutes per pound (unless you're doing without the stuffing—then it's 15 minutes per pound). Baste your bird with pan drippings or melted butter every forty-five minutes or so, but do it quickly so that the oven doesn't lose heat. During the last hour, remove the foil from the breast. The bird is done when a thermometer inserted in the thickest part of the thigh—but not touching bone—registers 175 to 180 degrees F. Then it's time to cut the bird (see Skill #80, Carve a Turkey, page 144).

**TIP: Rodgers prefers to do without spice rubs. "Spices can burn over the time a turkey is in the oven. Even if you try to put spices and butter under the skin, you're not going to get even distribution. Especially if you buy organic or free range, you should enjoy the taste of the turkey. Save the spices for the gravy."**

# 85 · COOK A LOBSTER

Next to cocktails on Ted Kennedy's boat, eating a boiled lobster is the ultimate New England experience. But you don't have to be in Hyannis Port to enjoy that experience. As a matter of fact, you can re-create it right in your own kitchen. All you need is a live lobster and a large pot (you can buy a stainless-steel wonder with a lobster basket, but really, all you need is a basic 20-quart stockpot). Then just follow this easy routine:

1. Fill the pot about $3/4$ full of water. Add about $1/2$ cup of sea salt for each gallon of water and stir it in. (You can go fancy with white wine, lemon, and bay leaves, but do yourself a favor and be a purist. You're in this for the succulent taste of the lobster.)

2. Heat the water to a rolling boil.

3. Now's the time to step up. Cut the rubber bands on your dinner's claws and grab that critter by the body. Put him head first into the water then cover the pot.

4. Cook small lobsters under two pounds from 17 to 20 minutes. Larger lobsters should go for about 20 to 25 minutes. The lobster's ready when it's bright red. If you're unsure, test by pulling off one of the small walking legs; the meat inside should be white, firm, and opaque.

**TIP: Lobsters' dance partner on the dinner table is a ramekin of drawn butter. Melt a stick or two of butter over low heat until it foams a little and solids sink to the bottom of the pan. Skim the foam, and pour the butter through a cheesecloth to filter out the solids (or just pour off that clarified golden liquid if you have a steady hand). Slice a few lemon wedges and your New England feast is ready!**

# CHAPTER 6

# SURVIVING THE GREAT OUTDOORS

**M**aybe you're no Grizzly Adams, but a baseline knowledge of how to handle yourself in nature is never a bad thing. Even if you restrict your wilderness activities to the occasional day hike and a little car camping, you should be familiar with basic outdoor survival skills.

When it comes to the great outdoors, the basics often come down to just that: water to drink, something to eat, shelter from rain and cold, and protection from things that go bump in the forest. Getting away from it all can often mean getting away from those things we have come to take for granted, like ready sources of food and a soft place to sleep.

Just the same, with a little ingenuity—and the time-tested insights of the professionals that we've gathered here—all the challenges that nature can put in your path are handily overcome, leaving you to relax and enjoy the wonderful world the Discovery Channel has made so famous.

# 86 · PITCH A TENT

Sleeping outdoors with a view of the stars is a wonderful idea . . . until the wind, rain, and cold hit. That's when you begin to really appreciate the advantages of a roof over your head. With modern technology, it's easier than ever to enjoy a little protection from the elements, even while deep in the wild. The answer is a tent.

Julie Hignell, program director for Outward Bound, is no stranger to tents. Her first concern is location. "First, look for a level site. Remove sharp objects from where the tent floor will sit (and other detritus, too). Make sure you're far from tall trees that might pose a threat in the event of lightning or have large limbs that could fall on the tent. Also avoid tree roots that might conduct electricity from lightning."

Once you're set with the site, Hignell suggests laying your ground cloth then constructing the tent carefully to prevent problems, especially with wind. "I always put my back to the wind and use it to my advantage in putting the tension on. As you're putting the tent up, note which way the wind is blowing and position the door facing away from the wind (or the door that you're going to use, because some of them will have a door on each end)." Make sure your ground cloth is completely covered by the tent. Otherwise, rain could collect on your ground cloth and soak the bottom of your tent.

In most cases, you'll be using a dome tent with poles that are shock corded together. The first step of construction is to put the long poles up, which may involve just giving them a shake, stretching the shock cord and popping the poles in place. The poles run corner to corner, through sleeves or loops, and hold the shape of the tent under tension. Hignell offers this insight: "A small detail that will ensure you're happy with the tent construction is to make sure that the floor has no wrinkles, with equal tension all the way around. That helps the pole system and the shape of the tent to do its job." Finish off with the rain fly, making it as taut as possible.

**TIP: If you haven't pitched a tent since your Cub Scout days, do a dry run in your backyard or living room. You can't drive the stakes into your hardwood floor, of course, but you'll get a feel for how the rods snap together without aggravations like poor weather conditions and hiker's fatigue.**

# 87 · CONSTRUCT A LEAN-TO SHELTER

When in the wild, we all need a little home away from home. But if you failed to bring a tent, you'll need to create a place to call your own—and nothing's easier than a lean-to shelter.

Mike Marcon, training director for Safe Return! Wilderness Emergency Care and Survival Training Center, says it starts with a "space blanket." "A space blanket is just a lightweight-polymer reflective sheet, sold in just about any outdoor equipment store. Space blankets are so cheap and light that you can carry five or six of them in your utility pockets." Of course, every smart hiker also packs some rope for emergencies just like this.

According to Marcon, the goal of the lean-to is to keep you dry and warm, whatever the weather, critical requirements if you're forced to spend an unscheduled night in the woods. That's why he recommends first building a hiker's best friend: a fire. For foolproof instructions, see Skill #88: Build a Campfire, page 162.

Marcon explains, "My approach is to get a fire going both for physical warmth and emotional comfort. Then shelter; in terms of basic shelter, a lean-to is fast and easy to build." He describes the process: "Select two trees with relatively flat and smooth ground between them; there should be enough space so that you can comfortably stretch out. Find a piece of dead fall long enough to span between the two trees. Lash it to the two trees about three feet up from the ground. Finish the shelter by lashing the space blanket to this cross-brace, and then staking the blanket to the ground with sharpened sticks." Or, for an even sturdier shelter, lash two long, sharpened sticks to the crossbrace, then stake the blanket to the ground with the sharpened ends.

**TIP: Didn't pack a space blanket? The branches of any coniferous tree will make a good roof, too. First lash a piece of deadfall between two trees, as described above. Then, beginning at ground level, arrange several boughs row by row, like you are arranging shingles on a roof. Be sure that the brush ends face down and the boughs overlap; this will help the rain slide off your shelter.**

# 88 · BUILD A CAMPFIRE

To find dry fuel, look for standing deadwood and broken branches stuck in tree limbs, says Tom Laskowski, director of the Midwest Native Skills Institute. Place the material next to your cheek; if it feels cool, it's too wet to burn efficiently. To fuel a 1-hour fire, gather two large fistfuls of tinder—such as cattail down and crushed pine needles—and about 30 twigs, 20 pencil-size sticks, and 10 wrist-thick pieces (1). Form a tepee with three 6-in.-tall sticks and place smaller sticks on the floor as a platform for the tinder. Lean the smallest sticks on the tepee, leaving a doorway to face the wind. Place the next size of sticks on top; repeat twice (2). Pack the tepee with the tinder and light it. Slowly add the 10 largest sticks in a star pattern (3). Grab the marshmallows—it's time for s'mores.

**TIP: Many a campfire has been foiled by wet matches. Be sure to pack your matches or lighter in a tightly sealed zip-top plastic bag or waterproof dry sack. If it's raining, for a foolproof fire starter, Laskowski recommends a cotton ball smeared with Vaseline (or Chap-Stick).**

# 89 · KEEP YOUR FOOD AWAY FROM WILDLIFE

All bears are kin to Yogi when it comes to campsite food. Other wild animals are just as hungry, so it's the wise outdoorsman who keeps his grub in a safe place.

And the safest place, according to bear expert Chuck Bartlebaugh, director of the Center for Wildlife Information where he oversees the national Be Bear Aware and Wildlife Stewardship Campaigns, is far from where you sleep. "The ideal is to locate your sleeping area about 100 yards from your food storage, prep, and eating areas."

The simplest solution is to hang your edible supplies from a tree. Bartlebaugh recommends, "Suspend your food in a waterproof sack at least 10 to 15 feet off the ground." He advises that the sack be hung about 4 feet from the branch on which it's hanging, and 4 feet from the side of the tree. "Use a good sack from a backcountry store and parachute cord. Just tie a little sinker over one end and gently toss it over the support by making a half-moon motion to get just enough momentum. Tie off the line around the tree."

You can also buy a specially made bear-proof container, but Bartlebaugh advises that even this type of container should be hung. "The last thing I want to do is have a bear play with it and chase it off somewhere, down a hillside or into a creek, never to be seen again—I'm kind of fond of food out there."

Lastly, don't bring food or beverages—or scented products of any kind—to the sleeping area at night. That's just an invitation to creatures you don't want sharing your sleeping bag.

If you live anywhere close to forest land or are fond of the occasional woodsy hike, you know the drill: long pants, light-colored clothing, and a thorough check for ticks once you're back inside. Still, ticks are awfully small blood-sucking creatures and there's always that chance you'll find one attached to you. Warm, moist locations are the draw, so be sure to check your armpits, groin, and hair.

Lyme disease is always the worry with ticks, but if you find and correctly remove the tick within a few hours, your chances of infection are greatly reduced. First, use tweezers to grab the tick by the head, as close to the surface of the skin as possible. Don't grab the body or you'll likely squeeze bacteria into your system and leave the head behind. Now pull with a firm and even pressure until the tick releases (it may take minutes). Pull straight away, and never twist the tick. Drop the tick into a jar of alcohol, and wash the site of the bite with alcohol. Finally, watch for any signs of infection (red circular rash, fever, fatigue, achiness), and if you experience any, take the tick and yourself to your doctor to check for Lyme disease.

**TIP: Although it's a tedious way to remove a tick, tweezers are the only reliable method. Never use petroleum jelly, a match, toothpaste, or other "ingenious" home remedies to remove a tick.**

# 91 · TIE THE PERFECT KNOT

If you want a versatile knot that can serve to tie down
tents or secure just about any guy line you'll need in a
campsite, turn to the trusty Coast Guard. "The bowline
is the king of knots," says Ben O'Brien, petty officer second class, U.S. Coast Guard. "We use it for almost everything: hauling buoys out of the water, tying up boats;
you name it."

Most people learn it by envisioning rabbits coming
out of holes. "At boot camp we didn't talk about rabbits," says O'Brien, who was the last active-duty keeper
at the famous Boston Lighthouse. To learn the Coastie
method, you first must know that they refer to the tail
of the rope as "the bitter end," and the rest of the rope
as "the standing part."

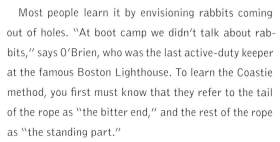

"Hold the bitter end in your right hand, and the stand-
ing part in your left. Now make a 'six' with your rope. The bitter end rests over
the standing part in the six. Next, feed the bitter end through the 'six' from
underneath. Take the bitter end around the backside of the standing part, then
back down the small hole, and tighten." You're ready for duty.

"You can tow a ship with a bowline and still get the knot loose afterward—
that's called 'breaking the neck,' and it's almost impossible with other knots.
I love that knot."

# 93 · MAKE A RAFT

. . . . . . . . . . . . . . . . . . . . . . . . . . . . . . . . . . . . . . . . . . . . . . . . . . .

Whether you need to cross a body of water to return to civilization, or simply envision lazy days floating downriver, your own homemade watercraft is the answer.

Paul Jones, North American regional manager for Global Vision International, describes finding the right material for your raft. "A reliable raft is usually going to be made of fallen timber. Dry logs are significantly lighter, and thus easier to get to the water's edge. They also have greater buoyancy (at least until they become saturated). If the raft must last, it's best to look for timber rich in oil or resins (think cedar, fresh pine, et cetera)."

Once you have collected 10 or 12 logs of similar size, ideally at least 8 ft. long, you need lashing material. Jones advises, "Use whatever you can for cordage—tough vines, twine, tent guy ropes, or even fishing line. Vines are ideal but any plant with long, strong, sinuous, flexible stems can be used. The young, outer fibers of some trees (just under the bark) can also be knotted and twisted together into rope in a pinch. Use as many different lashes as possible on each joint to increase the chances of your raft holding together." Instant incentive to carry an ample supply of parachute cord in your pack.

He suggests the following construction process:

1. Use at least half a dozen logs per person. The best two logs—thick, strong, straight, and ideally water resistant—form the underframe. Lay the remaining logs out side by side, alternating the taper of each log if they are tapered. The raft should be an evenly balanced rectangle with even weight distribution.

2. Place the underframe logs across the deck, about 8 to 12 inches from each end of the shortest logs in your raft and perpendicular to them. If you have nails or pegs, use these to secure the central few timbers of the deck before lashing the rest of the raft together. Make sure the logs are wedged tightly. If your lashing materials are limited, make sure the center of your raft is as secure as possible. If things go wrong, you can survive losing a log or two from the sides of your raft, but you want the core to be as solid as possible.

3. Add reinforcement. A diagonal brace or pair of braces across the underside will prevent the raft from twisting. If you have timber to spare, add an extra log alongside each brace and another log balanced along the joint between them. If your raft needs to carry two or more people, a pyramid of six logs along each side of the raft is almost essential to provide the necessary stability and buoyancy.

**TIP: Jones adds, "For added buoyancy, people often overlook the man-made materials they have with them. Dry bags filled with air, tarps, and waterproof jackets can all be used to create air pockets. It's easy to capsize if all your weight is at one end and the buoyancy is somewhere else, so think about where you need the support."**

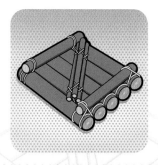

**The underframe** should be formed with the sturdiest two logs, then smaller logs can be lashed on a diagonal. This will prevent the raft from twisting.

# 95 · PADDLE A CANOE

For flat-water cruising, the stern-man's J-stroke is key: It keeps the canoe tracking in a straight line. Reach forward so the "catch"— the start of the blade's pull through the water—is well in front of your knees. At midstroke, the blade should be vertical and fully immersed. The upper arm extends diagonally across your body as though delivering a cross-punch and finishes on the outside of the gunwale (top edge of the canoe). The motion delivers power through a lever action; use the shaft hand initially as a fulcrum, then pull back on the shaft. The second half of the stroke traces the hook of the letter J. When you draw the blade out of the water, the power face (the side pulling against the water) is parallel to the canoe, with the thumb of your top hand pointing down. Your paddle is acting as a part-time rudder.

**TIP: Before you can paddle the canoe, you have to get into it. There are as many methods as there are canoeists, but in general reliable canoe-boarding involves keeping your weight over your center of gravity (i.e. widespread legs, no leaning) and keeping your center of gravity low (i.e. knees bent as much as possible with butt kept as low as possible).**

# 96 · SHOOT A BOW AND ARROW

The great outdoors is the perfect place to play Robin Hood, but just as with a gun, safety should be consideration one when shooting a bow and arrow. Shoot in an area clear of people and animals, ideally with a high burm (a solid embankment of compacted soil) for the target.

To be on the safe side, Jefflyne Potter, National Archery Association level 2 coach, advises that you leave 50 yards clear behind the target. Remove jewelry and loose clothing, and secure hair. It's best to wear safety equipment such as arm guards and finger tabs. Potter says, "I prefer arrows 3 or 4 inches longer than your fingertips when the butt of the arrow is placed at your chest and your arms are extended fully in front of you, palms together holding the pointed end."

She suggests the following process when you are ready to shoot:

# 97 · SET A SMALL-GAME SNARE

You aren't going to find any restaurants out there in the wild, so you better know how to catch your own sources of protein in a pinch.

Cliff Hodges, owner of Adventure Out, LLC, suggests the novice woodsman might want to use the "rolling snare," a basic trap that can be set to the size of the intended prey. "You use this on a 'run,' which is basically an animal highway," he explains. "Just like humans drive to work on the same road everyday, animals tend to stick to the same set of trails."

A successful snare starts with the right location. You have to have a good sense of the fundamentals of tracking, and read the ground for animal tracks and signs of fresh activity. Hodges explains why: "A rolling snare should be set on a freshly used run, and the trapper must know what kind of animals are using the run, so he can set the snare at the proper height and with the right amount of force to make an effective kill for that particular animal."

To set the snare, bend a sapling over so that the tip is almost touching the ground. Then, as Hodges describes, "Hook the sapling onto a stake driven into the ground, by carving a notch on each piece of wood so that the two pieces will grab on to each other. Make this junction as hair-trigger as possible so that the snare quickly releases when an animal triggers it."

He continues, "Attach a cord to the sapling and snake it across the ground until it reaches the run. Hide the cord as much as possible. The end of the line is tied with a slipknot to create a loop that will constrict around the animal's neck when pulled tight. Then prop your loop up using sticks at the appropriate height to reach the head and neck of your particular prey, and your snare is ready to go."

Set as many snares as possible because, as Hodges is the first to point out, catching prey this way is not easy. The variables make this a situation that requires experimentation, practice, and patience. Hodges says, "If I'm in a true survival situation, I would set at least six snares to ensure that I have dinner on the table that night. Check snares twice a day because most animals travel at sunset or sunrise."

**TIP: Hodges suggests "Camouflage! Animals are smart and tend to notice anything that is not natural. I cover my cord and notches with mud or dirt so that there is nothing in the area that looks manmade. I'm also careful to handle everything as little as possible and leave the premises as quickly as I can. Human scent can linger for quite some time and animals will definitely pick up on that."**

# 98 · FIND FRESH WATER

There's never a rain cloud when you need one. That's why it pays to take water with you into the wild. But if, like many inexperienced hikers and campers, you've underestimated your water needs, you'll have to find your own rain cloud substitute.

Tony Nester, owner-director of a unique wilderness skills school called Ancient Pathways based in Flagstaff, Arizona, advises swinging into survival mode. "The first thing is to conserve your own precious water in the form of your sweat. Don't go aimlessly hiking; sit down and gather your head, and really look at the landscape. Try to get to a high vantage point. Shiny reflections in the distance may sometimes lead you right to a water hole or a spring."

Of course, vegetation is a giveaway as well. Nester explains, "Look for bright intense green, such as cottonwoods or willows. Sometimes, with a cottonwood, you can dig down near the roots and find water." If you're in a more arid region, don't worry. Nester counsels that even chaparral and desert can hide water sources. "Look at the lay of the land for drainages that face north. That's what we use a lot out here in the desert, even where it hasn't rained in five or six months. You can often find water in little pockets, holes in rock depressions."

Finally, look for the wildlife itself. "Animal or insect life usually means there's water around. If all of the sudden you notice butterflies and humming birds, or see some wasps flying around, you're close to water—a little spring or a mud hole." Nester explains. "Animal tracks are a good sign, too—they can sometimes lead to a lake or spring."

**TIP: If you're worried that the water you find in a dirty hole might be a parasite's hot tub, consider the alternative as Nester describes it: "Here's the thing—you can't do without water. Whatever you might catch can be cured and probably won't even begin to affect you before you make it back to civilization. But there's no cure for death by dehydration."**

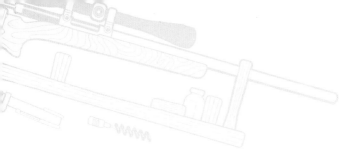

# 99 · CLEAN A BOLT-ACTION RIFLE

· · · · · · · · · · · · · · · · · · · · · · · · · · · · · · · · · · · · · · · · · · · · · · · · · · · ·

We won't teach you the fundamentals of deer hunting—that's beyond the scope of this book. But here's how to keep your piece clean as a whistle. Even if it never sees any big-game action, you'll be proud to have it hanging above your mantelpiece.

**1.** Make sure the rifle is not loaded.

**2.** Lay the rifle in a gun vise or cradle that will hold it securely during cleaning.

**3.** Remove the bolt and insert a bore guide in the action to protect it from being dinged by the cleaning rod. If the rifle has a scope, keep the scope covers on.

**4.** Spray foaming cleaner down the bore; let it stand for 10 to 15 minutes.

**5.** Screw a pointed jag that matches the rifle's caliber on the end of the cleaning rod. Soak a cloth-cleaning patch in a bore cleaner or solvent, then place it on the jag. Push the patch all the way through the bore from the action end. Always clean your rifle in only one direction—from the action to the muzzle. Never scrub back and forth. When the patch exits the muzzle, unscrew it, carefully draw the rod back out, and screw on a fresh patch. Repeat at least twice.

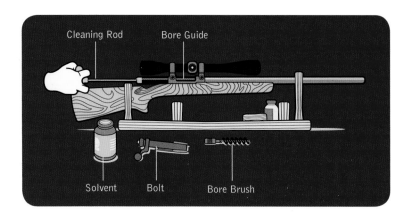

Cleaning Rod    Bore Guide

Solvent    Bolt    Bore Brush

**6.** Attach a bore brush to the cleaning rod and push it down the barrel three times to push grime and dirt out of the rifling grooves.

**7.** Replace the jag and run dry patches down the bore until they come out clean.

**8.** Spray a cleaner/lubricant on a cloth and wipe down the bolt body, bolt face, and the interior of the receiver. Before you replace the bolt, look through the barrel from the action end to be sure that it is clear of obstructions. Be sure to store the clean rifle in a secure case or gun cabinet.

**TIP: For maximum accuracy, clean your rifle thoroughly after every use, whether you fired a single round or hundreds. If you miss a shot, you'll know poor aim (not an obstruction in the bore) is to blame.**

# 100 · CATCH AND GUT A FISH

You don't have to be wildman Bear Grylls to find your own dinner on a camping trip. The trick lies in some basic knowledge of how to lure a fish onto your hook.

Catching the big (or not so big, but still cookable) one starts with the right equipment. In the case of a beginning angler, that means a modest rod-and-reel setup. According to Frank P. Baron, author of *What Fish Don't Want You to Know: An Insider's Guide to Freshwater Fishing*, "You should invest in a 7-ft. medium-action spinning rod, with a reel spooled with an 8-lb. test line. Tie on a size 6 bait-holder and hook, and pinch a couple round, split-shot sinkers a foot above the hook." (If this sounds like gibberish to you, don't worry, the sales guy at the sporting-goods store will get the drift.)

For bait, Baron recommends that the novice turn to the ever-popular and widely available nightcrawler. "Hook a fat one near the collar and you're ready for business," he says.

From there, the process as Baron describes it, is fairly straightforward. "If the bottom is clear of hook-eating obstructions, cast out your crawler and let it sit for a minute or two. Then drag it slowly back toward you a few feet at a time, pausing frequently."

Of course, Baron understands better than most that some lakes are messier than others. "If the bottom is messy, you need to attach a float or bobber above your bait to keep it from being fouled."

Then wait for the big moment. "When a fish bites, give it a little slack line, wait a few seconds to ensure it has a firm grasp on the bait, and yank to set the hook," Baron says. After that, reel in your dinner.

Baron suggests an overcast day or shady spot for the best fishing. "Fish hate light, so pray for cloudy weather and focus your efforts around dusk or dawn. If you have to fish in bright sun, cast your bait close to overhanging cover, such as weeds, or fish in deeper, darker water."

Once you've reeled in a keeper, Baron suggests the following process to gut and clean the fish:

1. If the fish needs to be scaled (not all do) rake a dull blade from the tail toward the head to remove all the scales. Be careful to keep your fingers safe, because some scales are sharp enough to cut you.
2. Slice the fish open, cutting the belly upward from the anus to the head.
3. Remove entrails, gills, and fins. Removing the head and tail is optional. ("I always remove the head," says Baron. "Those reproachful eyes. . . .")
4. Wash out the body cavity, and rinse the surface of the fish, too.

**TIP: Baron suggests that, if you want to save the fish for later, keep it cool but not damp. Pat it dry and wrap it in foil, plastic wrap, or, if opportunity permits, fern leaves, then store it in a cooler or refrigerator.**

# ART CREDITS

Illustrations by Stislow Design + Illustration except the following:

Gil Ahn: 165

Burcu Avsar: 69, 95, 114, 124, 141, 147

Dogo: 78, 79, 92, 93, 138, 152, 162

Thorsten Jochim/Getty Images: 171

Friedemann Vogel/Getty Images: 40

Hellobard & Intoaroute: 59, 86, 87, 97, 140, 146, 166, 167, 172, 181

Merle Henkenius: 63, 64, 76, 96

iStockphoto: 16, 18, 20, 22, 28, 32, 39, 60, 91, 94, 98, 99, 103, 107, 108, 113, 116, 121, 128, 132, 134, 150, 155, 158, 178, 182

Spencer Jones: 110, 111

James Pratt/Transtock/Jupiter Images: 101

Tim Klein/Workbook Stock/Jupiter Images: 118

Colby Lynse: 81

Punchstock: 80

George Retseck: 56, 57, 58, 74, 75

Transluszent.de: 53, 68

CSA Images/Veer: 3

James Westman: 85, 90

# INDEX

# A SOLVE-IT-FAST GUIDE
# FOR YOUR HOME

**Popular Mechanics**

## WHEN
## DUCT TAPE
## JUST ISN'T ENOUGH

## QUICK FIXES FOR
## EVERYDAY DISASTERS

$12.95

ISBN 978-1-58816-565-7

# ENVIRONMENTALLY SOUND HOUSEHOLD IDEAS THAT MAKE GOOD ECONOMIC SENSE

**Popular Mechanics**

## WHEN CHANGING A LIGHTBULB JUST ISN'T ENOUGH

HEATING   HOT WATER   COOLING   LAWN AND GARDEN

ROOF AND SIDING   GADGETS   STANDBY POWER   CAR CARE

150 WAYS TO SLASH YOUR HOUSEHOLD BILLS & SAVE ENERGY, TOO

$14.95

ISBN 978-1-58816-748-4

# REDEEM TODAY!
## One year of Popular Mechanics

# SUBSCRIPTION CHECKLIST

☐ *Fill out subscription card*

☐ *Include original receipt*

☐ *Mail back to Popular Mechanics*